T0285897

DREAMER

DAMI IM

DREAMER

hachette AUSTRALIA

hachette
AUSTRALIA

Published in Australia and New Zealand in 2022
by Hachette Australia
(an imprint of Hachette Australia Pty Limited)
Gadigal Country, Level 17, 207 Kent Street, Sydney, NSW 2000
www.hachette.com.au

Hachette Australia acknowledges and pays our respects to the past, present and
future Traditional Owners and Custodians of Country throughout Australia and
recognises the continuation of cultural, spiritual and educational practices of
Aboriginal and Torres Strait Islander peoples. Our head office is located on the
lands of the Gadigal people of the Eora Nation.

Copyright © Dami Army Pty Ltd 2022

This book is copyright. Apart from any fair dealing for the purposes of private study,
research, criticism or review permitted under the *Copyright Act 1968*, no part may
be stored or reproduced by any process without prior written permission.
Enquiries should be made to the publisher.

 A catalogue record for this
work is available from the
National Library of Australia

ISBN: 978 0 7336 4907 3 (paperback)

Cover design by Christabella Designs
Cover photography: front cover, Georges Antoni; back cover, Laz Smith.
Picture section photography: page 3, top right and middle, courtesy of FremantleMedia Australia
Pty Limited; page 4, top, courtesy of Waldemar Stoffel/Alamy Stock Photo; page 4, middle,
courtesy of TT News Agency/Alamy Stock Photo; page 4, bottom right, courtesy of dpa picture
alliance/Alamy Stock Photo; page 6, bottom left, courtesy of Tracey Nearmy/AAP Image;
page 6, bottom right, courtesy of Darrian Traynor/Getty Images; page 7, bottom, courtesy of
Patrick Hamilton/Getty Images; page 8, bottom left, courtesy of Jane Dempster Photography/
newspix; and page 8, bottom right, courtesy of Tanha Basile, Winni & Mini Photography.
All other images courtesy of Dami Im's personal collection.
Typeset in Sabon LT Std by Kirby Jones
Printed and bound in Australia by McPherson's Printing Group

 The paper this book is printed on is certified against the
Forest Stewardship Council® Standards. McPherson's Printing Group
holds FSC® chain of custody certification SA-COC-005379.
FSC® promotes environmentally responsible, socially beneficial and
economically viable management of the world's forests.

To my love, Harry

CONTENTS

Prologue

I'm on stage, but it's not in a concert hall or a theatre. This is a live show, but I'm not performing to the sort of audience I'm used to. I'm wearing a costume and it's far more elaborate than anything I'd usually perform in. That's because this stage is in a TV studio, and instead of playing on a piano – the instrument I'm used to performing on, that I've been learning since childhood, that I even have a university degree in – I'm about to sing.

This is the grand final of the 2013 season of *The X Factor*, a television show broadcast around Australia on Channel Seven. There are four celebrity judges: Dannii Minogue, Natalie Bassingthwaighte, Redfoo and Ronan Keating. Dannii has been my mentor since the early stages. But not at the earliest stage.

I almost didn't make it here. In fact, it looked like I would definitely never make it here. After a successful audition and getting through to the next round, I stumbled on the song I was given to sing and I was sent home.

Weeks went past. Months, actually. I went about my life, teaching piano in Brisbane, being newly married to my husband, Noah, performing as a singer on occasion. I'd hoped that *The X Factor* would help me find more work as a singer, because it was what I loved to do. Even one appearance on that show would be great. I had two. And I had to be satisfied with that. Or so I thought.

I received a phone call asking if I'd like to come back to the show. My immediate answer was yes. And once I was back, I completely embraced the experience and what it offered: the amazing costumes, the sets, the musicians we would perform with, the chance to be mentored by Dannii. As well as the utter exhaustion of the regimen of learning and rehearsing a new song each week, on that studio stage I also had to learn everything there is to know about being on television, which was completely new for me. Some days I was so tired I had to choose whether to eat dinner or sleep. Sleep usually won.

By the day of the final I have made it through several rounds performed live in the studio and to the television audience. I've harnessed all the musical experiences of my life – performing to all sorts of audiences – and everything I have learned from my music teachers since I was a child in South Korea. But at no stage has this felt like it is my destiny. That it is inevitable, somehow. I have worked to get here, I know that; I also know that I'm here by the grace of God, by the goodwill of the audience, by the faith put in me by so many people. I have never and will never take any of that for granted. My determination today is to do the best I can to honour that grace, that goodwill, that faith.

So when the lights dim and the opening bars of 'And I Am Telling You I'm Not Going' begin, I feel the power of that within me. I take a breath, start to sing, and let the music carry me away, as it has done since I was a very small child in Incheon, learning how to sound out notes on a piano.

CHAPTER ONE

Made in Korea

I was born in Seoul, the capital city of South Korea, and I grew up in Incheon, which is a city in itself, near where the international airport is now. Seoul is in the north of South Korea, close to the border with North Korea and the demilitarised zone (the DMZ, as some people know it).

I had a grandfather who left North Korea in 1948 just before the border closed. The split between the two Koreas also forced splits within many families, as it did in my own. My grandfather crossed the border carrying a pack of dried squid to sell and to eat. He believed he'd be reunited with his family soon, when things between North and South calmed down – then they shut the border on him.

I never met my grandfather. He died before I was born. His story can feel like it's very distant, from another country, but it's my own bloodline. And it's terrible for that to happen to one man, one family, let alone all the other families it affected. My grandma doesn't talk about it that much; my mum said they rarely discussed it until I asked them about it as an adult. It's an undercurrent of our family story, the way it would be for so many people.

My brother and I grew up learning about how sad the situation was in general, with the split between North and South. As kids we were aware that there was family over there for some people – including ours – and also that we were all Koreans but we weren't able to see each other.

There used to be special reunions agreed on by the North and South Korean governments where around a hundred families from each side would be selected by lottery to be reunited for the day. The whole country would cry watching the TV broadcast, as they saw families sobbing and hugging one another. They would share gifts and spend the day in a designated function hall, then at the end of it say goodbye and board separate buses to go home, crying uncontrollably, knowing it would be the last time they would ever see each other.

Back then everyone believed we should be reunified sometime down the track, but nowadays people have increasingly grown cold on the idea of reunification as they believe the cultural divide's become too significant. I still believe Korea should be reunited for all those families.

I only thought more deeply about the situation with North Korea and my granddad once I was an adult. When I was a kid it was just what it was and a lot of people had similar situations with their families. We believed it was something that happened in the past but it didn't hugely affect us in the present.

Australia is an island and Korea has a land border, but South Koreans feel like Korea is also an island because the border with the North is impenetrable, so it's not as if we can travel by land and find ourselves in a different country. We are surrounded by water otherwise.

So when you're in Korea you don't really see the border, which is heavily guarded by the army on both sides – the only reason to attempt to go through it is tourism or if you are serving in the army, which is mandatory for boys. The first time I had to look at it was with Dannii Minogue in 2014. After *The X Factor* we travelled there with a whole camera crew – my *X Factor* win had attracted so much attention from Australian viewers that the *Sunday Night* program on Channel Seven wanted to produce a story on me and my background, involving my life and my family in Korea. Dannii Minogue, my mentor on *The X Factor*, was the host of the segment so she joined us on this trip. We visited various places, like the playground I used to spend time in as a child in Incheon, went to a shimmering K-pop concert in a crowded stadium, and shared a homely feast at my grandma's house.

Visiting the North Korean border was one of the items to film. It seems bizarre that I had no idea until then, but that's when I realised just how close it was. It was twenty minutes up the road from where I grew up. I realise that saying this might make me sound dumb, but most Koreans would relate. Everyday citizens of Korea rarely feel the physical closeness to North Korea because of the emotional distance we feel due to the political situation between the two sides. It's a common experience for a Korean person to be shocked when they realise just how close North Korea really is.

When I visited the border with Dannii, it was the first time we got to take Grandma to see the North side. She was eighty-three and fragile, and Mum pushed her on a wheelchair up onto the lookout point overlooking the North Korean land that somehow appeared so peaceful. I felt emotional as I've never had any conversations with her about this. Grandma became pensive and very sentimental. She didn't say a lot but I could sense that she was feeling something deeply. This was where her late husband came from; the rest of his family lived there and she never got to meet them. As she looked down at the other, forbidden, side of Korea, she said very quietly under her breath, 'How I wish the two sides would unite again.'

It was a new experience for me, Mum and Grandma. None of us went there as a family, not only physically but with our conversations. For Grandma, there are things that only she knows and we don't know because we don't talk about all those kinds of things. As a family we tend to move on and don't get emotional. So when we actually had that opportunity, it was intense. It made me realise that there is so much we can never know about the people we love the most, nor they about us. And that some experiences are too painful to share; we can't force anyone to talk about them.

My childhood memories are all in Incheon. My parents, brother Kenny and I lived in an apartment and I went to kindergarten nearby. In Korea you start school the year you turn seven, so there are a few years to fill before that. There's no official preschool system in Korea but most children go to kindergartens. So I went to several kindergartens before starting school. And while some children love it, I wasn't one of them.

When I was really young, I cried all the time. I was scared of everyone who wasn't my mum and dad. That meant Mum couldn't send me anywhere. She told me later that she'd had to wait till my younger brother turned three to send me to kindergarten. He was too young to even speak properly, but the only way to get me to go was to send him with me. In other words, even though my poor brother was too young for kindergarten, he had to go because I was so scared and neurotic.

To this day, any kind of new environment or meeting a new person is more confronting for me than it is for most other people. I get tense and cautious. That probably means I'm naturally an introvert, and if that's the case it makes sense that at a young age I wanted to stay at home and not have to go to that new school and meet other children.

Sometimes I look back at that time and think, *I was born this way!* Nothing happened to make me like this, and certainly I was too young to make up reasons about why I didn't want to go to school. Not wanting to go was my instinctual response.

People are born with different temperaments and personality traits and that stays with us for life. We can't change that. But I have opened myself up to a lot of experiences in my life, some quite adventurous – going on a televised competition, for example. I don't see doing that kind of thing as denying my nature so much as accepting it and still pushing ahead with the challenges a new experience brings.

Even to this day when I have to make various decisions, my personality remains the same. My manager will ask me, 'What's your gut instinct on this matter?' or, simply, 'Do you want to do this?' My immediate impulse is always not to do whatever it is – 90 per cent of the time my first response is to run away from it and stay inside the warmth of my house and everything that is familiar to me. But somewhere along my childhood years I've learned not to follow my 'gut instinct' immediately but to pause and ask myself, *Is this worth pushing through?* And if my brain recognises that it's worth it, I'll do it, even though I don't want to. That will be the case for something that's hard or scary – if I can see the merit in it, I will do it and I will absolutely commit to it.

Feeling that impulse to run away from something then pushing through and doing it has been my resolve for everything.

So I've established that I was quite shy at school – but I also liked to have my people. I had two close friends and I would boss them around. They were the people I liked and was comfortable with. Around other people I was never the centre of attention but whenever there was a chance to perform in front of the class, I would take it.

In my first year of primary school we all learned the recorder – you probably did too, and I think most adults thought it was a horrible instrument! I remember the first time we all had to perform the exam piece, or whatever it was, in primary school. Santa Claus had given me a yellow plastic recorder for Christmas when I was five, and I was so excited to get the chance to show off and play at school.

I practised the recorder piece all day, every day. And then on the day of the exam as I watched some of the other kids play, I realised that I had been playing the instrument the wrong way around. The left hand was supposed to be on top, not the right hand. I could have just played it that way and done a good job. But on the spot I chose to change my hands around, which didn't produce good results. It was embarrassingly bad. The next time we did an exam, I made sure I did a lot of practice in the correct way so that I would play the best, because I was also a show-off and I wanted the recognition.

Another time, it was the end of school year and the teacher sat the whole class down on the floor and said if anyone wanted to perform they could raise their hand and share their talent with the class. Everyone was hesitant. Nobody put their hand up and there was just silence in the air. My seven-year-old introverted heart started to pound. I shut my eyes out of fear but stuck my hand up like I was in a movie. I stood in front of the whole class singing 'Silent Night' in English with a thick

Korean accent. I had learned the song from one of my friends. It was terrifying but once I had finished singing I felt fantastic.

So I was really shy and neurotic, but I still had that instinct to want to perform and show off. I don't know what that feeling is, but I just wanted to be in front of people, even though you'd think, with my introverted nature, that I'd not want to do that.

Maybe from a young age I had a sense that there is a performer's persona that can be separate and different from the core of a person. It's almost like I knew how to play the role of a performer, although I wouldn't have known to describe it that way.

I think I wanted to do it because I knew I could. As terrified as I was, if I didn't raise my hand I knew I would regret it. There were plenty of kids who didn't sing or perform and I don't think they cared, but for me it was a case of *I have to suck it up and do it now, or I'll regret it afterwards.*

I loved performing in front of my mum and dad and my cousins, and at home I would get up and sing. Many kids do that, but I really, really liked getting the glory. My mum did a lot of filming on her brick-like nineties camcorder and I've been able to watch some of that footage. One time she filmed me and my brother, Kenny, as she was asking us who wanted to sing next.

I put up my hand for the gazillionth time, then I stood up in front of the living room wall and sang another song sounding pretty mediocre, in a way only a mother could appreciate. You could hear Mum talking from behind the camera, saying, 'Give Kenny a chance!' But I never wanted to. I was greedy for praise and the spotlight.

I should say that my brother *is* musical, but he's not like me in that he doesn't love attention. He's a quiet achiever. I needed glory and attention.

Performing does run in the family, though, as my mother is an opera singer. I recall she gave a big recital at one point; I remember her going to rehearsals and going to see her pianist to rehearse. And she had dress fittings too – she had a big green dress and a purple dress. This was in the early nineties and the dresses had big, puffy sleeves. I loved looking at the princess dresses that I'd seen in Disney movies but I didn't necessarily think that what my mum was doing was amazing and special. I thought that was what everyone did. Play music and perform.

There was a lot of music in our house all the time. My parents both loved music. Mum would sing and I would harmonise. Dad would play the guitar and the keyboard. Music was so natural for us.

Mum and Dad met at Seoul's Yonsei University. Mum majored in classical voice and Dad in engineering. They both joined a club on campus that was for students who loved 'recreation', which was about leading games and activities for groups of people. Dad said he fell in love with Mum when he first heard her sing. He loved music and people who were talented in music!

As a kid living in Korea, I loved singing too and thought I sounded pretty good. And no-one told me otherwise. But then as I grew a bit older, around ten years of age, Mum would say, 'Kenny has a stronger voice. You are more like Dad, your voice isn't as strong.' I had this really hoarse voice and I'd lose it all the time. I was loud and I yelled, and then I would lose my voice. A classically trained singer would never let their voice go hoarse like that. So Mum thought I didn't inherit her pipes.

There was often opera playing in our house but Mum also took me to symphony orchestra concerts and the ballet – although I used to fall asleep during those. Poor Mum!

We also listened to pop music, including the Korean pop songs Dad liked back then, and the old pop songs by bands such as the Carpenters and Simon and Garfunkel that my parents grew up listening to. There was also gospel music, the praise and worship songs from church, the Sunday choir music. That was more for my dad. He loved music. He still does. So he'd try to learn his part for the choir, and all that was going on in the house, too.

Once I was a bit older I'd find out about new pop groups from kids at school. Two of my cousins were girls who were slightly older than me; they were super cool – at least, they were to me at the time – they wore colourful headbands with dangling faux earrings attached at the ends! And they would know all the music and all the cool stuff, so I'd pay attention to what they were listening to.

I remember getting totally obsessed with one band when I was still in Korea. I was quite young, in Year Three. The group was called JuJu Club. All my cousins would listen to a lot of pop music, as in K-pop, but they listened to everything that was on the charts. Whereas I'd get obsessed with one group or one band, and when you love music like that you want to hear all the B-sides from that artist and know their whole story. I wanted to hear everything the group had recorded, not just one song.

So I'd listen to a cassette tape again and again. I would look at the lyrics on the cassette and memorise every song. Then I would perform the songs in front of our families. And my friends and I had a private tutor for English at one point and I would make them all sit through my performances.

So JuJu Club was my first musical obsession. Then there was another K-pop performer, one girl called Bo-ah Kwon, known professionally as BoA, who I got really, really obsessed with when I came to Australia. Her songs were the ones that I used to practise and sing.

I wasn't aware of too many K-pop artists while we still lived in Korea. I was a bit too young for any of that – I was still watching *Sailor Moon* and other cartoons. But I knew there were the cool kind of teenager TV programs where the hippest bands would come on and perform in their nineties attire.

Apart from my forays into playing the recorder I was always tinkling on the piano as a kid; there are videos of me playing. I started lessons when I was five. At that time, where we lived, it was trendy to give kids piano lessons, violin lessons, things like that. So I was the same as everybody else, basically. All my friends played piano too. Everyone played the same music, like Beethoven and Mozart. There was a set repertoire and we all played it, which, looking back, seems very strange. Korea was so densely populated, there were so many kids, and we all went through the same regimen. The learning pathway was very rigid, possibly because it had to be when there were so many children to accommodate.

I remember taking part in a mass competition – hundreds of kids played in it. I was given a silver award, which is not as much of an achievement as it may sound. Hundreds of kids got the gold and hundreds of kids got the silver. I was just one of many!

When I was in Year Three I auditioned for the school recital and somehow I was selected to be the one pianist to do the performance in my year level. I don't know what the teacher saw in me because everyone else played superbly.

My family were so thrilled that I would be doing a recital, although I remember being so shy and feeling so awkward on stage. I had my head tilted the whole time and when I bowed, I bowed with an ear on my shoulder and everybody laughed.

You could think of learning piano as a kid job, I guess. I didn't hate it, but then I didn't love it either. It was just alright. But I didn't like Mum telling me to practise every day. I do remember even as a young child having that feeling of dread: *Oh, I have to practise.* Because doing something every day is hard when you're that age. And I certainly couldn't do that anymore now I'm a grown-up with choices.

I remember thinking, *I wish I could have a break today – just today.* My mum wasn't super scary and strict like some mums ... but she was firm. She'd say,

'Dami, you should practise. You haven't done your practice.' Sometimes I'd do a short twenty-minute session. At other times I'd go longer than an hour. But having to do something every day – that took a lot of self-control. I have to admit that it definitely helped me for life – it taught me discipline and the importance of repetition in learning something new.

Given that all the children I grew up with in Korea were learning instruments, perhaps it's no surprise a whole genre of pop music, K-pop, emerged from Korea. So many of us were trained to be musicians from a young age – and singers too.

Most Koreans can sing in tune, and you can't say that about too many other cultures. That was one of the things that shocked me when I first came to Australia. At school assembly we sang the Australian national anthem and most of the kids were tone deaf! I had never experienced that in my life. I thought, *What is happening? They can't sing in tune!* It was a huge eye-opener for me.

I think the exposure to music and singing makes a big difference in Korea. From a young age Koreans love to sing and are exposed to a lot of singing. I didn't realise at the time but it's simply part of our culture.

Speaking of piano again: even though I didn't like the lessons and the practice, there was something about learning an instrument that I must have enjoyed because I also wanted to learn the violin. I begged Mum to let me learn violin and play at school and get lessons.

I remember that was after Mum and I had a little fight about me not wanting to practise piano, and I cried. The next day she said, 'Your school's offering these violin group lessons. Do you want to do it?' Which was her gesture of reconciliation with me. I think it was her way of saying, 'Okay, you can do violin if you're so sick of the piano.' And then I had to do both ...

There was definitely a lot of interest for me in learning a new instrument and I eventually picked up the flute too. No-one told me to do it. I just wanted to learn it and practise and practise.

I kept playing violin throughout high school, which was in Australia, and I kept up the flute and played it at different stages. I played in the school orchestra. Even at university I was majoring in piano but I joined the university orchestra to play violin.

Violin was always an instrument I played for fun whereas piano became a job, essentially. Piano involves a lot of exercises and scales, it's not only playing a lovely piece. And, of course, you can't get good at something by just enjoying it. Enjoyment comes later when you become good at it.

In hindsight I'm grateful that my parents made me learn the piano and that my mum stuck around to make sure I practised. Even when I was grumpy and didn't want to put my heart into it I always sat down and did it and ticked it off. That sense of duty, I suppose it was, that kept me there would pay off when I was older and pursuing music as a career.

CHAPTER TWO

Stressful Paradise

*W*hen I was young my parents would sometimes take me and my brother on overseas trips, especially to New Zealand. My uncle – my father's younger brother – lived in Auckland for a number of years before he moved to Brisbane, so then we'd come to Australia to visit him and his family.

Each visit was only a few days long. So when we went to Brisbane in 1998, I thought it was going to be another one of those short trips. But then a few days turned into a few more days. We were living with our uncle and his family; they took us to the zoo and to feed the kangaroos and see the koalas and go swimming all the time. My brother, my two cousins and I had a great time. It felt just like a holiday, even though we were there for much longer than usual.

Then the school term started and that's when I realised what was going on: our visit was, in fact, a permanent stay. We went to the shops, and I said, 'Mum, I want to buy this colouring book.'

'No, no, no,' she said, 'you don't have time for that. You have school.'

I replied, 'What do you mean?' And I was thinking: *I don't get to keep playing? What's happening?*

So that's it, holidays were over. We were preparing for school. And we lived in Australia now!

When I was younger Dad's family business involved running a factory in Incheon, where we lived. They were expanding the business, and that meant moving to a regional area in Korea, which means we moved there too. However, Mum and Dad didn't want us to grow up there.

Education is very important in Korea, and very competitive. I believe my parents thought that if they were going to move away from Incheon, where education was very good, to an area where the system wasn't as strong, the future for me and my brother would be bleak. So both my dad and his older brother decided, well, why don't we take this opportunity to send the kids away? That's why my cousins were in Australia as well, because Dad's younger brother had already made that decision.

When we left Incheon to move to the regional area my parents said, 'We're going to move there for a bit, but we're going to send you overseas and Dad's going to stay.' So I said goodbye to my school friends and to my old life, although I don't remember feeling that sad, and I don't know if I would have felt differently if I'd known that this move was a precursor to leaving the country.

Our parents' initial plan was to send us overseas for a couple of years to learn English, because that was something a lot of Koreans were doing, sending families or children away to learn English and then come back, so they would be that much further ahead in their education.

Our move to Australia was meant to be temporary but we ended up all staying because my parents really loved us being here.

Dad visited almost every school holidays, for a week at a time. And then during the summer here, the winter over there, we'd go back to Korea. I think we went back every year during the summer. For a while, my memory of Korea was winter. That was all we experienced for ten years or so. Korea to me was always cold and the trees never had any leaves.

We did that for a long time, although Dad never moved here permanently. I think he was able to come here for longer periods of time but that was after years and years had passed. He was always just going back and forth, then when we were in high school he tried to stay here for longer periods of time. I think it's just the way the company was set up. He was able to leave a bit more to other people to run it.

When I was in high school he was able to come for a month or longer at a time, which was much nicer. I remember him coming for a week and after the halfway mark he'd always start counting down the days until he had to go home and he was sad about that.

Now I think about it, it would've been really, really hard for both him and Mum being separated like that and Dad living by himself. He's not functional by himself. He can't cook. He just eats random stuff when he's by himself. He needs to be cared for. And it wasn't easy for Mum, being by herself. She had my auntie nearby but bringing up your kids overseas with limited language and knowledge, it would've been really hard.

I think that's why the Korean church community in Brisbane was a huge help for her. For other families, too, for that matter. Everybody felt safe there. There were people speaking the same language, eating the same food, and in the same boat trying to live in another country and trying to understand how it works and all of that. Our lives were centred around the Korean church because it made sense. That was our community.

When I began school in Australia I couldn't speak English. It was a small school and there was one class per year level from preschool to Year Twelve. Being at a school that small was completely new to me because in Korea there were eleven classes in my year level.

It felt like we were in a little country town. All the kids looked different from what I was used to – they were blonde or brunette. They were trying to be nice to me and take care of me, but I also didn't understand what was going on.

A girl called Karen was assigned as my buddy. I met her on the first day and she took me around and showed me everywhere and helped me. But the second day I came back to school and I couldn't find her. I was going up to girls and saying, 'Karen? Karen?' and they were not Karen! To me everyone looked the same. I couldn't tell them apart. She had to come to me because I couldn't find her.

I hear all the time that Asians look the same and people say, 'How do you tell them apart? You have the same eye colour and hair colour.' Apart from this being an insult it makes me frustrated when someone says this because it's such a misunderstanding. We don't look at eye colours or hair colours. In fact it took me a while to notice people's eye colours. Koreans and other Asian people look at different facial features and shapes. Whereas when I saw these Australian kids, the features that I was looking for were all over the shop. I wasn't used to how they looked. Which meant they all ended up looking the same. They all had light hair and lighter, bigger Caucasian eyes.

Of course my brother, Kenny, was going through the same challenges. Even today he'll sometimes bring it up. He's pretty introverted too – he doesn't even like calling to order pizza. He blames it on the fact that we were thrown into this environment where we knew nothing and we had to survive. My cousins had had a similar experience when they moved here.

I think we all processed it differently. One of my cousins was more extroverted and he just went out running, playing soccer – he was more into sport. I'm sure he had his difficulties and challenges, but he seemed fine. Whereas I wasn't as fine. And music was one of the ways I dealt with it. It's interesting that we all came at the same time, around similar ages, but each of us dealt with it differently.

In such a small school, as the new kid who couldn't speak English, I felt like I stood out more than I would have in a larger school, and that's not necessarily a good thing when you're a child – you don't really want to stick out that way. Unless I was performing.

At one point the whole class wanted to come and help teach me English. Which was nice, but also a little bit embarrassing. It was a big fun thing for everybody but I was a neurotic kid who was scared of everything. I was sensitive. I felt like I had spikes on me when things weren't familiar, like I was a porcupine.

It took a while to get used to being at that school because it was very different from what I was used to, but I found that interesting. It was hugely stressful for me but I had fun at the same time, as odd as that may sound. The kids would go out at lunchtime and catch lizards and I liked that. You'd never do that in Korea. I'd never even seen lizards before, but kids were catching them and running around on the lawn all the time. I didn't have access to a big lawn area in Korea, it was all buildings and concrete. But this was sunshine and pools. It was like stressful paradise. *Wow, it's lovely, but I'm so scared!* That's what I was always thinking.

Among all of these new experiences I was learning a new language too, which was also stressful, but overall my time at that school wasn't completely bad. I made friends there.

We lived in a two-storey townhouse with a couple of rooms in a quiet suburb called Runcorn, which is on the south side, about a half-hour drive from the Brisbane CBD. In Brisbane you are either a south-side person or a north-side person. Asian people are generally south.

These days Runcorn has become a big Asian hub, but when we arrived in 1998 the area wasn't well known.

Brisbane was warm and where we lived we could hear cicadas, lots of insect noises and birds. And if we just walked around the block there was the townhouse pool and we had access to that all the time. When you're a kid, things like that make the day fun. I'm sure it was more stressful for Mum to have to deal with the bills and the forms and so on, but my job was to just try to get used to everything.

And some things were constant: I was still practising piano and violin. Music was always playing in the house. In some important ways, it wasn't different at all from what we had left behind.

CHAPTER THREE

Piano Girl

hen I arrived in Australia I had already been learning the piano for about four years. I didn't think that being able to play the piano was anything special because every other child in Korea seemed to play, although I realised pretty quickly that the same wasn't true in Australia. That was one of the cultural differences – one of many – that I noticed.

I started taking lessons with a teacher at my primary school in Brisbane and she was really impressed with what I could do. She recommended that I audition for Young Conservatorium, which is a program run out of the Queensland Conservatorium of Music, for gifted children who play instruments. Mum took me to audition at the Conservatorium, where I got to play a big grand piano.

We had an upright piano at home, but a lot of pianists dream about playing a grand piano. When I first played it at the audition the touch felt a bit heavier than the upright I was used to. I needed more finger strength than I normally used. I didn't struggle, but it did feel like it was the next level up from what I was used to.

Having that upright, though, gave me an advantage because some of the kids who learned piano at school had keyboards rather than pianos, because the lessons were given on keyboards. There's a difference between the way a piano feels to play and how a keyboard feels. And I'll be honest: if you're serious about playing piano I don't think it's a very good idea to learn on a keyboard. At that audition, the children who had only ever played on a keyboard struggled trying to play on a grand piano. The mechanisms of a real piano are intricate and complex. As a child it fascinated me to open the lid of my upright and look at the felted hammers strike the triple strings as I touched the ivory keys with my fingers. Pressing the pedal and seeing every hammer move from side to side. Tinkling the highest keys and listening to the glistening notes ring out. A great piano player would know how to control their fingers and their whole body to understand how to produce various tones – strong, light, deep, resonant, short, long, firm or gentle. I believe you need a real piano to be able to learn all that. I realise that not everyone can have a piano, but besides the technical aspects, there's also something romantic about having a real instrument in your house.

Later my parents did buy me a grand piano. When I started entering eisteddfods and competitions, I entered a big national competition called Yamaha Piano Competition. Every state held the competition and the winners would be flown to Sydney to compete on a national level. I won the Queensland heat and needless to say, my parents and I were just thrilled. That's when they decided to get me a Yamaha grand piano. It was the next step up from an upright piano and an unspoken way of signifying that I was serious about being a pianist. Buying a Yamaha was also good marketing by my parents! And I still have that Yamaha C5. It was a very wise investment. And very expensive. But my parents happily invested in this instrument with hopes that their daughter would be on track to becoming a world-renowned concert pianist.

My audition to the Young Conservatorium was successful. After I got into that program I began lessons from teachers who taught at the university, Joyce Bennett and Jung-Eun Byun. They were really lovely and very good at what they did.

Apart from learning from the best teachers, another benefit of being part of the program was the access to performance opportunities. At the end of each term we were to perform at a recital with all the other children enrolled in the piano course. Often it would be at the Ian Hanger Recital Hall at the Conservatorium which was always nerve-racking, but my most memorable was when I got to perform in Queen Street Mall, in the centre of Brisbane's CBD. It was a big deal for a ten-year-old girl from Korea to be doing that, performing Chopin, Rachmaninoff and Bach, composers like that, in a big public place.

I attended the Young Conservatorium until Year Twelve. It was a lot of extra work on top of school, as it wasn't a school replacement – everything I did there was in addition to school. It didn't feel like it was too much, though. It became normal to me and I was proud to be in the program. I loved going into the big Con building. I felt special.

Kenny played the saxophone, but he did that at school so Mum didn't have to take him elsewhere for lessons. We both had various after-school activities. With English being a second language for us, Mum found an English tutor to try to give us an extra boost and help us read and write. I also attended many school band and orchestral activities. After school and even during school holidays we had concerts and competitions and extracurricular activities that Mum had to drive us to.

Competing became a fixture in my life. I remember the first time I did an eisteddfod was the Redlands eisteddfod, when I was ten or eleven. By then I was at the Young Con and my teachers' other students were doing eisteddfods. One of the girls brought her trophy to lessons – she'd come third in some competition. Her parents spoke to my parents about it at a recital, saying how proud they were.

I thought it was pretty cool that she had a trophy. So my teacher signed me up for my first eisteddfod. In each one we could enter ourselves in multiple sections – one section would be baroque music, another would be sonatas, for example. These sections were basically multiple competitions within the one eisteddfod. I did four or five of those at my first eisteddfod.

The concerto section is the most difficult, because when performing a concerto, a pianist plays as a soloist with an orchestra accompaniment. And a concerto is generally a grand and challenging piece of composition. We didn't have an orchestra there, obviously – another piano accompanist played the orchestra part on a second piano and I played along with that piano.

I started winning first prize in so many categories, including the concerto section, to the point where it felt like if I didn't come first it would be a disappointment for me and my parents!

The competitions were held in these little classroom-sized rooms. As a young musician it would make me feel so nervous and my palms would sweat. At the end of all those entries there was a final awards night and there was this very prestigious award called the Most Promising Pianist Award. It was given to one young pianist from the entire eisteddfod with all the sections combined. There was even some money attached to it, like a hundred dollars, which was a significant amount for a young kid.

As all the finalists and winners were announced, I was looking up to the girl who won third place, thinking, *Oh my gosh, it must be so nice to win a trophy.* But I was doing so well too. That was when I thought for the first time, *I can win. I'm really good at this.* It was so encouraging and a real revelation to me and my family when my name was called out as the winner. It was the first time my family thought, *Wow!*, because we'd been so impressed by the girl who'd won third place.

From then on I entered more competitions; year after year, Mum – and Dad when he was in Australia – would drive me to these. I was always so nervous before performing and competing. It's not fun, but the thought of winning something at the end of it all *is* fun. But you never know until you're done, of course. It was my eternal tension of not wanting to do something but knowing it could be good if I did it well.

I felt confident after that first eisteddfod, but it's hard to know who the better player is, because it's a very subjective thing. So I could think that another pianist is better than me but the judges think differently, and it can be true the other way. Somehow some people win all the time and other people don't. And for me the reality was that I kept on winning.

The element that is hardest to quantify is talent – lots of kids could work hard but talent was that extra element that judges at a competition might be able to identify. My family, myself included, are on the conservative side and underestimated my capabilities. It took me a while to accept that I was in fact lucky enough to have natural talent. All throughout high school, playing piano wasn't that hard for me. I practised every day but I wasn't practising eight hours a day like some genius kids did. I did one hour – two if I was motivated. And that's not a lot compared to so many of the others. But I still kept winning competitions.

I even remember when I was doing violin at school, the violin teacher liked me but also was annoyed at me at the same time because I never really practised and I wasn't a hugely focused student. Playing violin for me was purely for fun.

The violin teacher organised a competition at school with a guest adjudicator, and I ended up winning that even though I didn't practise much for it and I wasn't getting lessons from the teacher – and obviously it was her students I beat. It seemed as though I didn't work as hard as some of the other kids but I was getting results. To be fair, I don't know how much practice the others actually did at home, so who knows, perhaps they didn't work that hard either, but they were definitely more serious about it.

That's what made me think, *I have no choice other than to become a pianist because it's a gift. So I just have to do it.* I didn't feel as though I had the right to not do something with the talent I had. I didn't ask to have that talent, which made it feel like it wasn't mine to squander.

I practised piano every single day through all of my childhood and youth. Some days were better than others and some days I didn't feel like practising and I would feel sorry for myself. Still, I always felt guilty that I didn't practise as much as I was supposed to, which was more like four to eight hours a day rather than the two hours that I did. That amount was bearable for me and I could get away with it. I was still winning and was far ahead of most players in Queensland. However, there came a time when I couldn't do that anymore.

When I got to university I was still at the top of the music major, winning prizes and receiving high academic results, but when I decided to go to the next level of performance – an international competition – that's when I realised I needed to put in more time to practise. In a typical international competition you'd have to play, say, seven different pieces. Some of these have three movements, which go on for twenty minutes each. This means the program is two hours long, and it's not as though you can practise for two hours to learn a two-hour program. You have to practise every waking hour for *months* for that. So from that point on I thought if I didn't love this and love practising all day, every day – which some of these international players were doing – it wouldn't be enough anymore.

The problem was that I wasn't willing to do it. Because, for as much as I felt like piano was what I *should* do, it wasn't what I *wanted* to do. The people who were destined to become concert pianists happily put in the hours; they were used to locking themselves up in a room, practising all day and night, and didn't seem to mind that level of commitment, whereas I didn't see the worth. I had better things to do. And I knew I didn't want that to be the rest of my life.

CHAPTER FOUR

My Famous Singing Teacher

*A*s a kid I not only enjoyed singing but I was quite confident about my vocal abilities. Despite Mum's view that I didn't inherit her vocal cords and my voice wasn't built as strongly as hers, I still thought I was quite good. That is until I played back my own recording for the first time.

I was in Year Eight when it happened. I was obsessed with BoA, the Korean singer I mentioned earlier. She became a megastar in Korea and Japan in the early 2000s with her powerful voice and her ability to dance while singing. She was the Britney Spears counterpart in Asia. I listened to her albums on my portable CD player and downloaded video clips of her performances, which I burned onto CDs that I stored in my disc folder. Remember those? I was simply obsessed with her.

Even though I idolised BoA, part of me believed what Dad always said about pop stars.

'It's all technology and effects,' he would say, 'anyone can sound good with autotune!'

Dad was an early adaptor and a constant learner back then, and still is to this day. He installed a program on his computer that you could record your voice on. He told me that if I had a backing track, I could record myself singing on top of that and use 'autotune' and other tricks to make myself sound good, just like BoA.

That sounded like fun to me. So I asked him to hit record and I sang one of my favourite BoA songs. We played the recording back. I didn't sound that great. In fact I sounded quite disappointing. I had no control in my voice. It was wobbly and you could hear me straining to reach the higher notes.

I waited for Dad to put on the magical autotune and whatever technological tricks he told me about. He played around with the program. Then he played it back to me. Still bad.

As time went on and as we went through more tricks and effects on the program, it started to dawn on me. No amount of technology would save my bad singing. The simple truth glared me in the face – my idol BoA could sing well, and I couldn't. How arrogant I had been!

This was a shocking revelation to me. But it was also the start of something that would change my life. I wanted to keep trying. Every day, I would record the song again. I would try different ways, like singing one verse at a time. Then one line. Then one word. Sometimes I would sing a single word fifty times till I sounded more like BoA.

This became my new obsession. Every day after school I would come home and lock myself in my room and record. I would try to mimic BoA's songs. No matter how long it took, and it took me weeks sometimes, I loved being able to finish recording a song from beginning to end. Even if they didn't sound as good as BoA, I didn't want to stop. It only made me determined to try again. During the holidays I would forget to eat and forget to go to the bathroom. I would record her songs one by one, and eventually other pop songs from others singers I loved listening to, such as Mariah Carey and Stacie Orrico.

I started to write my own songs and record them as well. I would create my own track in this software and make songs I thought would sound good.

When I was in Year Eleven I became friends with a boy at school called Hiro, who came from Japan. We met at choir – he was in the choir and I was the piano accompanist. He was also into making his own songs.

One day, he played me his new song at school and it sounded incredible. It was like a song you would hear on the radio.

We became really close and during the holidays I would go to his house and help him record his demo vocals. It was so much fun to record on his tracks.

Hiro went on to become a successful music producer in Japan, working with some big names that most people over there would know. And he's since told me that the one artist he's loved working with the most was none other than an artist named BoA. He told me how professional she was to work with when she recorded one of his songs.

I also got the opportunity to meet BoA in real life. It was when I visited Korea in 2014 with Dannii Minogue for the *Sunday Night* program. The team had arranged a surprise visit to BoA's studio at her company, SM. I had no idea when I walked into the building that I would be meeting the artist who had started everything for me all those years before.

I was half asleep after a long week of filming when I arrived there. I couldn't believe what was happening in front of me – I almost cried and had trouble joining words together. I did manage to sing in front of her the very first song that I recorded of hers. It was the song that made me realise that I was a crap singer, and I was praying that I sounded better by this point. I was so nervous, like a little child meeting her hero.

These days if people ask me whether I had a singing teacher as a kid, depending on who they are, I tell them that it was BoA, the pop princess of Korea. Or, that it was Dad and his computer that gave me a shock therapy.

CHAPTER FIVE

The Calling

*D*espite my conviction that piano wasn't going to be my life, it was the subject of my studies at the University of Queensland as I undertook a Bachelor of Music.

Max Olding was my piano teacher there. He was a fantastic educator; he passed away at the end of 2021, at ninety-two years of age. Everyone in the music world respected him and I did too, very much. You could see he cared about each of his students and he wanted me to push as far as I could with my music. He really believed in me. He would give me extra lessons if I needed more help, and he would drive me to places where I was playing. Once I forgot to take an extra piece of sheet music so he drove back and got it himself. There were countless tiny moments like that when his genuine love and passion for his pupils shone through.

Max was very dedicated to helping and giving everything for his students. When you do weekly lessons with somebody for four years, you develop a strong bond. During the lessons I would talk to him about piano and also about everything that I was going through. I was seventeen when I started lessons with him – still a young student. And we all have a lot of questions at that age.

I didn't know what I actually wanted to do. He knew I wasn't wildly keen on playing piano as my career and sole focus – but then he also knew that I was talented and it just came naturally to me. So he pushed me to do those big competitions with the two-hour programs.

After one lesson, though, he said to me, out of the blue, 'Hey, you are not just a pianist. You are a communicator.'

For some reason that gave me shivers right through my body. At the time, it felt like the voice of God, which may sound dramatic but I had been involved with the Korean Christian Church for several years by then and God was part of my daily life.

Part of my difficulty with the path I was on was that at this time in my life, I was always thinking, *What is my calling?* I suppose that was my church background. This was always emphasised so much in church: *What is the vision? What is it that God is calling you to do? Why did I end up here as a pianist after all these years?*

I was always wondering and thinking and agonising over what I needed to do. So when Max said that about me being a communicator, at that right time, in that moment, it was like God was speaking to me.

After Max said it I thought, *I'm going to remember that – I'm a communicator.*

For so many years after that, even after I'd left university, I kept thinking about what he'd said. *I'm a communicator.* Whether I play piano or not, with the music I make or whatever I do, I have to communicate. And at that stage I wanted to communicate God's message to the world. It felt like a calling, because I didn't just want to become a concert pianist like everybody else wanted me to become. The idea of being a communicator just resonated with me. And as time went on and I was singing and writing my songs, I always remembered that.

I don't know why Max said that. I didn't know where it came from. It was very profound, considering all I was doing was playing my pieces and probably complaining about how I didn't want to practise. It would've been after a lesson where I was saying, 'I don't want to do this,' because I said that a lot.

Max kept trying to convince me to do the competitions but I didn't want to do them because it was such hard work. For these competitions you have to memorise every piece, which meant I had to memorise two hours' worth of music.

To be honest, working on the music for those competitions was painful and I didn't love it. But in the end I did them because of him.

Max often seemed to have tears in his eyes because I didn't love piano as much as he loved it for me, and he could see the talent and the potential. He'd almost cry after each lesson. But it was in a really loving way. To me it felt like a parent saying, *Why don't you see your potential?* And even though I didn't turn out the way maybe he wanted me to turn out – as a concert pianist – I did end up pursuing music and becoming a communicator through music.

Several years later Max spoke in a media interview about me and he said some really lovely things. So I knew he was proud of me even though I didn't follow in his footsteps as such.

From high school all the way through university I knew that I was trying to reconcile the fact that playing piano seemed like it was my calling even though I didn't actually feel like pursuing it as a career. When I was in Year Twelve, trying to decide what to do after school, I always just imagined piano. I didn't even need to think about it, but that's when I did start to think about it. *I don't like practising, I don't enjoy it, but*

I guess I'm good at it. And I thought that's what I had to do.

Then my parents convinced me to do the course and get a degree in piano and then whether it's my calling or not, I can do something I want to after that. It was good advice in hindsight because it stays with me forever that I have an official qualification in classical piano. Otherwise I'd be like everybody else who played piano when they were young and gave up. I'm glad I listened to them.

At the same time, I knew it wasn't for me. Because some of the other students weren't 'naturally talented' or winning competitions with their instruments, but they loved it. So they would talk about music all the time. They would go and listen to other musicians play and they just breathed classical music. Whereas I wanted to get out of any kind of commitment or rehearsal. I found it boring.

Some of those people who were passionate about music ended up making some kind of career out of it. I can see now how that came to be: if you persevere and you try to do something with that passion, you will, you can. As long as you don't compare yourself to other people and get discouraged. And here's a little tip: I think people who keep doing it convince other people that they're actually good, even if they were just an okay musician who would benefit from more training. I've seen that so many times.

While I was at uni I made new friends. One of them was an international student from Japan who was also studying a music degree. For her birthday I wrote her a song, recorded it at home and gave it to her. It wasn't even that good but it was the thought that counted.

Apparently my friend had connections to some agents in Japan because she was doing some modelling whenever she was there. She sent the song to her agency and the next thing I knew, this man who was running a music management company in Japan wanted to come and see me.

He flew to Brisbane because he wanted to hear me sing in real life. Which didn't mean he would see me perform at a show or anything like that – we booked a karaoke room! So my friend and I joined this man, who was in his fifties, in a little karaoke room and I sang for him. It was definitely one of the strangest gigs of my life.

'It's good,' he said. 'Very good.'

I should say that at this time in my life I wasn't studying singing – that would come later – nor was I performing, apart from singing in church. So that means I hadn't even had a single thought about singing as a career.

He wanted me to fly over to Japan and audition for major labels in Tokyo. His company booked my flights and accommodation, and we booked a flight for my dad as well because I didn't want to go by myself. After all, I didn't know this man – or anyone else in Japan – so I had no way of knowing if the whole thing was legitimate.

I flew to Tokyo and was told that the management company had booked auditions at these incredible, high-end recording studios. They were massive with expensive recording equipment and could easily fit more than fifty people. As I looked around, I recognised names of famous Japanese pop stars. In one of these recording studios I would perform for major labels; Sony was one of them.

At the time I had a vocal nodule, as I had been doing a lot at church – I was the interpreter, which meant I talked nonstop, as well as singing. So I barely had a proper voice left in me. In addition, I was really unprepared as I hadn't known what to expect.

I was asked to sing some songs in Japanese and they wanted me to sing these hymns that I had recorded. It did seem somewhat random to sing hymns at an audition for Japanese record company executives but I went along with it, played piano and sang these hymns. I didn't know what else to do so I just did what I was used to doing – I didn't have a defined sound or even a specific genre I sang in. Which meant that the auditions weren't very good – although they were a good experience.

After I flew home none of those labels wanted to sign me, but the manager kept communicating with me about different opportunities, such as singing the Olympics theme song.

After a little while, though, I freaked out a bit because I didn't want to actually go to Japan and live there – for one thing, I didn't speak the language.

Another very important factor was that I'd just started dating Noah, who would later become my husband. He didn't like the idea of me going to Japan. And even though we'd only just started dating (I'll tell you more about him later, but suffice to say now that even though we'd just started dating we'd known each other for a while), his opinions mattered to me and I already was feeling less keen about the whole idea of moving to another country, so I decided to give that up.

The combination of those factors meant that I cut ties with that manager in Japan and we've had no contact since.

After I'd returned from Japan I still had the nodule in my throat. Thankfully I didn't need surgery, but I had to tell everybody at church that I was going to stop doing everything. I was leading the church band and translating for all the non-English members, as well as being the leader of several groups and different things, and all that required a fair amount of talking and yelling.

I went to my pastor and asked, 'What should I do?'

'You should pause all your commitments,' he said, 'and take a big break. Your health is more important.'

I hadn't been sure how people at the church were going to react when I said I was quitting so many activities, but they were kind, saying I should look after my voice because the problem was quite serious. So I just stopped using my voice as much and thankfully the nodule problem resolved itself.

Apart from that, it was time for me to take a break. I was pretty worn out, so it was nice to just be an attendee and observe for a while instead of being the one organising. Even so, I was still attending a lot of services. For me and a lot of my friends during that time, life was centred around church.

On Sundays, I'd be there from morning until evening. During the week there would be a small group catch-up or a meeting at someone's house. And then on Friday there was an evening service and we'd all have dinner together. Saturday would be a rehearsal day. So I think even though I stopped doing the speaking part, there were still plenty of things to go to and play piano for, because my piano duties didn't stop. I was still very much involved – just not using my voice as much.

Although having that many activities at church might seem like it was a burden, I did them because they were fun.

I was really dedicated to the church and I liked being able to serve, to make music and be a leader, teaching people. I was also a university student and that's a stage of life when you have more time than later in adulthood.

I also learned a lot about practising with a band, for example; about leading people – and being bad at it as well. About working with people. Nobody was being paid to be there because we were all doing it as service to the church, but that also meant I couldn't get upset if people didn't come to things when they were meant to. When people are volunteers you can't really force them to turn up, to practise for that church band or to be on time.

Most people would come to rehearsal not having practised and you can probably imagine that for me, given that I was studying music at university, this was quite frustrating! Then we'd rehearse and the next time they'd forget every single thing that we'd gone over. I had to learn how to be patient and not get too annoyed.

Overall I think those experiences helped me with a lot of my relationships as an adult and making sure I was treating people the way I would want to be treated. I learned a lot about organising events, being a leader, and I met a lot of really great friends there – including my husband.

The people I knew through church comprised my main social group, even though I was at university and meeting people there. While I was at school I had school friends as well as church friends but by the time I was at university most of my friends were from church.

Most of Mum's friends were also from church – because they're the people she met when she moved here. But for me, at university everyone did their own thing and people moved on to various courses and majors. And, as I mentioned earlier, I wasn't interested in the classical music side of things, even though that's what I was studying. So when the other students were socialising and bonding over some recital, I wasn't interested. I didn't want to be there. And so I'd just go to church.

It sounds like I was always trying to get out of doing the one thing I was at university to do, which was play music, although that wasn't the case and I always felt bad that I wasn't as keen as the other students were on recitals and competitions. I felt lazy, but I knew I wasn't lazy. I just didn't like the music. I also felt like I was letting people down.

Once I was put into a trio with a violinist and a cellist as part of a subject. We had to decide on a piece together and rehearse once a week, then perform at the end of the semester to be assessed. Like in all of my other courses, I did what needed to be done but I wanted to be involved no more or no less than what was required to get a good grade. On the other hand, the other musicians were far more enthusiastic. They wanted us to learn extra pieces and enter competitions together. They even wanted to travel interstate to do masterclasses and participate in different opportunities as a trio. I was just not interested. All I wanted to do was finish my course with good grades and move on.

Without that passion some of the other students had, it was hard to sustain that level of work without it feeling like drudgery. Being socially awkward had something to do with it too: I wasn't that close to the other students so I didn't have friendship as a motivation to make an effort with that trio. Pursuing a degree in something that I wasn't passionate about made forming friendships harder anyway, as they were constantly talking about composers from Stravinsky to Strauss, and I just had no interest. How could I tell them that I'd ended up there because I liked the recognition and winning but I actually didn't like the music that we'd been playing together? I didn't want to travel with people I only sort of knew. I just wanted to hang out with people I knew at church. I was more comfortable with my little sheltered life.

CHAPTER SIX

The Leap

*T*he final semester of university can be a distressing time for students as they start thinking about their lives out in the real world, but it is generally worse for music performance students. There's not a set path for a music performance major and it's not like anyone has a secure job lined up once they graduate. It was the same for me and I was worried about my future, but a part of me was looking forward to closing off this chapter of my life. Since I could remember, I had been practising classical piano every single day. I couldn't even imagine a life where I didn't have to do that anymore, but I couldn't wait to find out!

I also was looking forward to figuring out what I really wanted to do. Now that I had an official degree in piano and I'd gone as far as my parents wanted me to go, I could finally move on.

I wanted to get a master's degree in a course I was actually passionate about this time. By this stage I had been singing at church and gaining more confidence and skills as a singer, and I knew I loved pop and contemporary music. Also, while I was at university I wrote my honours thesis on music education in developing countries as I was interested in the power of music for underprivileged communities. I was torn between a degree in contemporary music performance and in education research.

After much thought and praying, I decided that now was the time to pursue performance. I figured I could choose to do education later in life, whereas performing was something I needed to try while I was still young. I had been playing classical piano my whole life, but popular music and singing had been just a hobby that I never had formal training in, and it was a risk to pursue this on a serious level. I didn't even know if I would be admitted into the course, but the time had come where I could actually take the leap into what makes my heart beat. I decided to audition for a Master's in Contemporary Voice at the Queensland Conservatorium of Music.

I had no idea even where to start so I contacted a church friend who had studied the same course and asked her for help. She gave me some tips and what kinds of songs to choose. I took her advice onboard and learned a few jazz standards and sang while playing the piano. Even though I was nervous, just like I'd been at any piano concerts in the past, I found the whole process fun because I was learning and performing songs that I enjoyed.

When I received the letter of acceptance I was beyond excited. It was the start to a new life and it was like getting official permission to follow my passion! I enjoyed being surrounded by music that I actually loved, as well as being around musicians who loved similar types of music. For the first time in my life, I received formal vocal training with some of the best teachers. It was like a dream.

While studying for my master's, I got the chance to perform at venues that were a little different from the formal concert halls I was used to. Every opportunity I had to sing at a bar buzzing with people enjoying their evenings, or a dimly lit Brisbane jazz club overlooking the Brisbane River, was a chance to learn and build confidence, and I absorbed everything like a sponge.

My first-ever paid gig as a singer was at a Chinese restaurant in South Bank. Initially I was paid to come in on a few nights to play background music on piano. One day I went to the boss with a suggestion.

'What if I sang one night a week? I'll bring my microphone and an amplifier.'

She loved the idea and advertised Thursday evenings as 'Shanghai Jazz Night'. She got me to dress in a blue silk cheongsam and sing jazz standards and old pop songs with a friend of mine playing the piano. It was a lot of fun and it didn't hurt that I was also getting paid for it! Some people would notice the performance and some would even give a tip. But most diners didn't pay attention – we were just background music. Sometimes I would turn my volume up and sing so loudly that the boss would come over and turn it back down. When she went away I would turn my volume up again. I wanted to be heard and noticed!

Eventually I finished my master's, and I had to decide what to do next and find work.

As one of my last projects at university, I made an album. It was full of songs that I had written, half in Korean, half in English, all with a Christian theme. And in those years before streaming was a thing, I actually had CDs made. Of course, CDs are still being made but at the time that was the only way to present your music to other people.

I had no idea how an album was made so I had to figure it out as I went and, to an extent, make it up along the way. It was part of my degree, so it wasn't optional. I asked the teachers at uni how other people did it, so I had some support.

I wrote all the songs for the album in Korean and a friend translated those lyrics into English. I organised a band of jazz musicians to play the instrumental parts. Everything was recorded at my church, which was nothing like a studio in terms of soundproofing and acoustics. It was very echoey, for one thing. But studios are expensive to hire and I was a student at the time, so the church was the best option.

The sound engineer I hired was used to recording live music so we recorded it like a live performance, which happens on some albums anyway. It means that all the musicians play together, just as if they were performing at a show. Normally what happens in a studio recording is that each track is recorded separately and you can adjust the sound for each to make sure it's as good as possible, and the vocal is recorded separately too. My vocals for the album were recorded separately to the band but everything else was live. If you listen to that album you can tell the recording is not studio quality, but we certainly did the best we could in the circumstances.

For the cover, Dad took photos in our back garden and my friend designed the artwork. The photos were fairly random – I was holding a globe and a fake watermelon – don't ask me why. I learned a lot during that whole experience and in the end I had an album in my hands, so I was really excited about that and proud that I had achieved it. I was giddy that I had made my own CD.

Dad wanted to help me promote the album, so he did some research online and sent CDs to radio stations and anywhere he thought might play my music. He found this Korean Christian online radio station called Wow CCM.

My dad had a meeting with Mr Kim, this man who ran the station – who, quite coincidentally, happened to live near him in Korea. And this man agreed to set up some promotions for me and my album. He suggested I come to Korea.

'We'll see if we can promote it on the station,' Mr Kim told Dad, 'and make some connections with other churches, and promote it at various camps and church services.'

So I flew to Korea along with Noah, and went to the studio to meet Mr Kim. Except even though I had the address I couldn't seem to find the place. It was in an industrial area with old and dusty bike workshops and metalworks. The whole area was very rundown and there weren't many people around. Safe to say it wasn't what I was expecting, nor was I comfortable there – in fact, it was a bit scary.

Just as I was starting to question whether it was the right decision to come here, Mr Kim arrived – we were in the right place after all.

The studio was underground, which was why I hadn't been able to identify it at ground level. We went down these little steps and there was the radio station, which was really just one booth behind glass and a big audio desk to control everything.

We had a meeting there, even though I was still feeling a little unsettled about the whole thing and worried about what I'd got myself into. But Mr Kim was really lovely and he was sincere about wanting to help me.

After that meeting he recorded some interviews with me and I would do a show with him, an online radio chat, every week. I'd sing songs or rearrange existing gospel songs and sing them. And we'd travel to different churches to sing and sell my album. It was fun, and not at all anything I could have known to expect. It was also my first taste of working as a gospel singer, even though I made very little money.

That initial foray into Korean Christian radio became a regular gig for me. I'd stay in Korea for a couple of months then go back to Australia and spend time with Noah, who wasn't able to come with me after that initial visit.

So just like my father before me, I spent several years going back and forth between Korea and Australia to do some work and all these activities promoting my music.

That work involved being invited to sing at church services – it might be to perform one song during the service or to speak and to sing at a youth event. There were lots of youth camps, churches and Christian media. I also sang at army base services and once visited a juvenile detention facility to sing as well. Each stint was fairly tightly booked.

Dad, and sometimes Mum if she was in Korea at the same time, would drive me to these places. Some of them were really far from the city – those youth camps would be held in some remote part of Korea, like the mountains. So there was quite a lot of travelling for us.

After I sang at each event Mum and Dad would help me set up a little stand and sell the CDs. Even though Dad was particularly embarrassed to do it, as most people walked right past the stand, my mum stood there selling the CDs that no-one cared about, just to support me. My parents were like my managers at the time with everything they were doing for me, and I was so lucky to have them there.

Those stints in Korea involved visiting a wide array of places – I never said no to anything. I'd go to these little country towns and sing in their churches, and as you might imagine their sound systems were not necessarily that good. I didn't have my own gear so I had to work with whatever was provided. My backing track would suddenly stop and there would never be anybody who could help me. Or the microphone would be tinny like those microphones on tourist buses. But that's all I had so I'd sing and do my best, even though I knew that microphone would make me sound like a fairly woeful singer.

What those shows lacked in technical quality, however, they made up for in what they could offer me in experience. I had the chance to learn a lot about what to do and, importantly, what not to do to ensure that the performance would be as good as possible. That doesn't mean I had stipulations – it meant I was thinking about the audience. If the set-up wasn't appropriate for the purpose it would be the audience who suffered most of all. Who wants to listen to someone singing on a tinny microphone?

So I learned that if there was no microphone stand and it was a gig where I needed to play piano, I shouldn't do the gig because I simply couldn't play piano and hold a mic and sing.

Once someone said, 'We don't have a mic stand but I'll hold the mic for you.' So they held it, but his arm was drooping down to my belly button and I had to keep chasing the mic while playing the piano and singing. It was an awful way to perform!

At one place they played my backing track through a TV screen, which was a terrible start – and then the CD jumped halfway through so the song went to a different spot. Nobody else knew that that had happened – they just thought I forgot where to sing.

I did a Christian TV show where they said, 'We will mix in your backing track at the end,' in post-production. They put it in the wrong spot, so it sounded like I was singing out of time the whole way through.

Through all of that I learned that there needs to be a minimum standard for a good performance – but it was hard to enforce that when I was a nobody! I was just grateful to get an invitation somewhere, even if they didn't pay me. That was my position at the time. I did everything just to get the experience and hoped that one day I could be in a better position.

I guess it also made me be grateful once I had the luxury to ask for some kind of minimal standard with my set-up. At the time I was just going with it and doing everything that I was asked to do – that was my attitude. And also being a Christian artist, you couldn't be someone who's picky or known to be a diva. At the time I felt like I couldn't ask for money or even ask about how many people would be there. I would still say yes and travel for hours even if there were only five grandmas in the audience.

In general my attitude was that I should say yes to every invitation whether big or small because I believed this was my calling. I didn't feel that I should pick and choose where I go. I met countless pastors and leaders who would serve in these smaller communities so selflessly and it was eye-opening to witness how some of these people lived their lives and gave themselves to the service of others without making much money. The whole experience was a constant learning one for me.

The music I was performing in Korea was all Christian and through that experience I learned how to sing songs that would connect with the audience in front of me. That meant learning how to adapt my set to whoever was in the audience. If it was grandmas in a country town who were over seventy years of age, I'd sing older, more traditional hymns and I wouldn't sing any contemporary numbers at all. If I was performing at a youth camp I tried to sing newer songs, and sometimes even slip in a K-pop song.

As a gospel singer, I couldn't just go and sing. I always felt I needed to be prepared spiritually as well because your job description isn't just to perform music but to teach people on a spiritual level. You are a minister – you're ministering to people with music and your speech. And that responsibility felt a bit heavy at times because

I thought of myself as a normal person who happened to have the gift of music.

That extra dimension to what I was doing required a lot of preparation. And by preparation I don't mean vocal warm-up exercises – it's preparing mentally for myself and the audience, and in a broader sense it was making sure that my life reflected what I was singing about and that I was prepared to be a spiritual leader. Looking back, that was quite heavy for a twenty-two-year-old to deal with.

These days, of course, because I'm performing different sorts of music it doesn't have that same responsibility to it. I still take my work very seriously but I can sing about my experiences in my music in a candid way rather than trying to send a particular kind of message or be a leader. This feels so much more natural to me.

In a way, that's why I wanted to become a secular singer – I just wanted to write and sing to share honestly. That didn't mean that I didn't want to be a Christian singer, but to be a gospel singer, or a Contemporary Christian Music (CCM) singer, I felt like the role was not to simply be a performer who is Christian but to be a minister or a pastor to the audience and I didn't feel like I fit that role.

I know a lot of CCM singers who love that role as a minister and live and breathe it. But it was clear to me, and stayed clear, that I just wanted to make music to communicate. And whether I sang directly about God or about another experience in life, as a singer I could do both without being put on a pedestal as some kind of religious leader.

But I spent two years doing that, learning how to perform to all sorts of crowds. This was experience I would apply later on, although I could never have known that then. What I'd had, though, was the sort of apprenticeship university could never have given me. Some performers come up through the pub circuit – I had the Korean church circuit! It was an invaluable education in how to put on a show and connect with the audience, and to communicate openly through music, even if I wasn't conscious of that at the time.

CHAPTER SEVEN

Noah Kim Kim

*A*ustralia was introduced to my husband, Noah, at the same time they were introduced to me: during my *X Factor* audition. Noah was standing at the side of the stage with the show's host, Luke Jacobz, and he was excited from start to finish. As he said then, he's my number one fan – and he has been for a while now.

Noah and I met when I was about thirteen years old and he was eighteen. We met at the Korean church I attended. We always had new people coming and going from Korea and he was the new person who joined us. Apparently he played baseball in Korea; he'd come to Australia to study English like most other Koreans who arrived in Australia at that time.

Noah became friends with my cousin who was living with me and my family. She is six years older than me and was studying English, like Noah, and they became good friends. So they would be talking all the time on the phone, and I was sharing a room with my cousin. She stayed with us for the duration of her studies, so we shared a room for quite a while.

Before I met Noah he had bleached his hair – so he had fairly ugly blond hair that was really light from the bleach. He was a little bit muscly, which I noticed. I was a teenager, after all! As soon as I saw him I developed a mini crush on him. Back then I had crushes on lots of people – as most teenagers do – but it lasted a long time.

I have to confess that at the time I thought his hair was perfectly cute – it's only now that I look back and think it wasn't such a good look, but it was a typical kind of late nineties, early two thousands bad Asian bleached hair. Technology has improved since then so that it's not so ugly and brassy, praise God for that!

I used to see Noah all the time at church because back then we were going to church at least two or three times a week. Then he'd come over sometimes with other people or my mum would invite kids over from church to feed them and things like that.

He gave me his email address so we could keep in touch, and we were emailing each other from time to time, just saying 'hello' and 'what are you up to?'

I used to really look forward to his emails.

Actually, it wasn't a mini crush I had on Noah. It was a full-on crush and it lasted for several years. He became really special to me. I don't think he had any idea about how I felt, though. As I mentioned, I was only thirteen when we met, and he just thought of me as the cousin of his friend, although he has since told me that he always felt there was something special about me and he wanted to keep in touch.

While Noah was living in Australia his circumstances changed. His parents had been supporting him financially while he was studying but at a certain point they couldn't any more – university fees were really expensive, as was rent and everything else he needed to be able to live overseas. So they told him to come home.

Instead, Noah decided to stay in Australia. In order to support himself he worked three jobs while still studying full-time; he ended up living at the church as a security person. During that time he was crazy busy and he was struggling, too, to make things work. I watched him go through that, because he was still in my friendship group at the time.

When I was in Year Eleven Noah decided to go back to Korea to finish his military service; it's compulsory for every Korean young man to serve two years in the military. I still had a crush on him at that time so I was really, really sad when he left. But I moved on and lived my life.

By the time Noah returned to Australia I was at university. And, as he said, by the time he came back I had become a young woman. So he asked me to go on a date with him.

I was very cautious. I wasn't in Year Eleven anymore – I was just turning eighteen. I didn't want to go through having a stupid, childish crush on someone again and I thought if I started spending time with him that would happen. But he was still really nice, just as I remembered, and I really liked that. He seemed really soft and gentle; one of those people who are just nice to everybody. But then when I actually talked to him he had this fight in him – that's why he was able to survive all those years with little money. He also had this big vision and a fire burning of wanting to do something great, to achieve his dream and also serve people. These two different sides to him were in contrast to each other but that made him really attractive to me – although I was still cautious.

This time around, though, he was the one who liked me and I didn't see it coming. After all those years of having a crush on him, then getting over it while he was away, it was amazing when he asked me out. I could have said no, because the ball was definitely in my court – but of course I was going to do it!

After all that time of knowing each other, then him being away, I don't know what the odds were of us finding each other again. Maybe it's fate or whatever you'd like to call it: there was something there, pulling us together, even though we didn't even know it at the time.

Noah didn't have his English name 'Noah' when he first came to Australia. He had people calling him by his last name, Kim, because most people couldn't pronounce his Korean name. One day one of his colleagues asked him, 'What's your name?'

He replied, 'Kim.'

'Then what's your last name?' they asked again.

'Kim!'

'So your name is Kim Kim?'

They were confused. For a lot of people from overseas, it's quite common to have an English name people can pronounce easily so they don't have to waste so much time correcting people.

'Kim Kim' asked me to help find him an English name. I suggested 'Noah', and explained that it's from the Bible. The one who built the ark.

'Great! It sounds nice and even better that it's also a character from the Bible.' He loved it.

But secretly I had just watched a movie that I absolutely loved. It was called *The Notebook*. It may or may not have been the name of the character that Ryan Gosling played. But anyway!

The Noah that people saw on *The X Factor* is Noah as he always is: super supportive of me and happy for any success I have. When I had doubts about whether I could continue my passion and pursue my career, even as I got older, he did not.

We started talking about getting married quite early on in our relationship. I guess it's different for a lot of people, but for us, in our communities, if you're dating someone you're dating because you are potentially thinking about marrying that person if it's right.

But we waited because I was scared that being married would change everything in a way I wouldn't like. I had it in my head that it would compromise my career and whatever I wanted to do, that it would change the way people saw me.

Noah would tell me things like, 'I really don't believe that God gave you the ability to sing so that you could sing while washing dishes or mopping the floor.' And he really meant it – he didn't believe that marriage should mean that I had to adjust my dreams or compromise anything.

'I don't see it like that,' he'd say. 'You've got a great talent. You have to keep doing stuff with it. You have to use it.' That was really reassuring.

Still, after we were married a lot of people *did* treat me differently, even though I felt exactly the same. I had just turned twenty-four and at church suddenly I was put into a different group. I still turned up to my young adults group because that's where all my friends were. But instead I was expected to go to the kitchen with the ladies who were in their forties and fifties and sixties. They gave me an apron and expected me to hang out with them instead of with people my own age.

That was, to be honest, terrifying. My biggest fear was of being put in that category and it happened straightaway – which I suppose means I was right to have been worried.

Even when I was on *The X Factor*, the other contestants who were eighteen or twenty would ask me things like, 'So, Dami, what's your dream? Oh no, hang on – what *did* you want to be before you were married?'

I couldn't believe they'd ask me that but it was further proof that people expected me to suddenly change myself and what I wanted in life simply because I was married.

Around the time Noah and I married I was still travelling back and forth to Korea for work. I'd spend a few months there and come back for a few months, and I kept doing that for a while. And when I was in Australia I wasn't getting much work as a singer, just odd gigs here and there sometimes at a pub or a bar. I was teaching piano and some vocal lessons, but then I had to leave after a few months to return to Korea.

Everything was so unsettled during that time, even though it was fun and new and exciting. When I was in Australia I would record and prepare music to take to Korea, and that kept me occupied. But after a year and a half it just became too hard going back and forth. I wanted to settle in Australia.

After I decided to stop travelling, that's when I started getting call-backs from *The X Factor*. So it seemed as if my timing had worked out well – not that I knew what lay ahead of me then.

CHAPTER EIGHT

The X Factor

*T*owards the end of 2012 I was looking for something to help me stay in Australia because I was getting more work in Korea. I wasn't sure what to do to be able to have a career in Australia, because when you're a musician or singer there's no one path into a career – often there's no path at all.

Even though I was in my early twenties I couldn't help thinking, *I'm getting older. I'm twenty-three and once I'm thirty, it's all over. So I'd better do something.*

As a singer, I'd often have people coming up to me saying, 'You should audition for *Australian Idol*, or for *The X Factor* or *The Voice.*'

A lot of singers would get a bit offended by that – and I was no different. Whenever someone would say that I'd think, *I'm already a singer. Why would I go on a TV show to prove myself? I've been a musician all my life.*

I don't need to do a silly gimmick on TV to prove that I'm an artist. That was my ego talking, of course.

But I started to wonder: *What have I got to lose?*

The answer was: nothing. I didn't have much of a career in Australia and I was too introverted to be able to schmooze my way into the right circles to get gigs. That's how other musicians were getting opportunities – by networking – but I didn't know how to do that. I didn't have any connections.

I decided to take a look one night. I looked up which shows were out there. I looked up *The Voice*, because I knew what that show was. I didn't even know what *The X Factor* was. I didn't watch it. But applications for *The Voice* were closed and the only show that was still open was *The X Factor*. I put my name down and I was given a date for the preliminary auditions in Brisbane.

When I arrived in the morning, I had to queue up along with everyone else outside a hotel – and it was quite a long queue. Once I was inside I was given a number and had to wait all day before I sang. In the first round I auditioned in a little conference room in front of some producers. There was no microphone, there was no accompaniment – not even a note to cue you. But they had to get through a lot of people so it made sense that there wasn't a big set-up for each singer.

I felt very awkward just standing there in front of the

producers and singing in a quiet room. But I have to admit that musically I had an advantage because I have perfect pitch, which means I can find my pitch without a note being played. I've had perfect pitch since I was a little kid in Korea. This is just one of those things that some musicians have and others do not. There are professional musicians who don't have it and amateur musicians who do. Having it is a great advantage and in that situation it was a strength.

The hard part was sitting around and looking at all these people with lots of make-up and funky clothes, thinking that they'd be far more likely to be chosen than I was because they looked the part. Then when I was finally called in I felt really small.

Some people were sent home after that first round but I made it through and then had to sing in front of another producer and a camera on that same day. I sang the same song as in the previous round and it was a song by Christina Aguilera called 'Hurt'. I'd shortlisted all these pop songs and learned them just for this audition, and finally landed on this one as I decided that this was a song that was popular enough but not a clichéd audition song that was overdone by every second person who walked into the room.

After singing the first verse and the chorus in a dry conference room, they said, 'We'll contact you.'

I went home – and then I went back to Korea for three months. I didn't hear anything from them in that time so I thought I hadn't made it through.

After three months, though, when I had forgotten about the whole thing, I got a call saying that they wanted me to go to Melbourne to be part of the TV auditions. It all happened really quickly and I had to be there about a week after that phone call. They said I could bring family and friends to support me and they'd fly me over. I didn't want to tell too many people about me auditioning, so only Noah came with me.

The TV audition had a lot of similarities to that original audition day, except that it was in a big arena and there were a lot more cameras and crew everywhere. We flew over on the first flight in the morning. We checked into a hotel, then we were taken to the arena where we had to join the queue along with hundreds of other contestants. I didn't actually get to perform until the end of the night, around midnight.

During the day I had to do a short interview – they filmed grabs with the contestants, asking what we did for work and how we were feeling. But mostly we were waiting around, which, as it turns out, is really tiring!

While I was sitting around I could observe everything that was going on and I could see that other contestants were receiving a lot more attention from the producers and cameras than me. Those people were more extroverted than I was and, well, I didn't feel very interesting.

There were people who Noah and I sat with all day – because it wasn't as if we could all move around to different spots. There was a girl who was with her mother and the mother was very keen to tell us how amazing her daughter was and how great she was at piano and how she'd done all these exams. I was sitting there thinking, *I did that when I was much younger, but I don't go around telling people.*

There was one guy who liked to tell us how great he was and then he'd start singing out of nowhere, just warming up, he said. And, really, everyone was a bit like that – there were so many characters singing spontaneously all over the place. And me, thinking, *Wow, everyone's so good. And they're all good looking.* So I really felt intimidated. I think Noah and I both felt somewhat out of place and a bit small at that time.

Being interviewed on camera wasn't my favourite part of the day. I wasn't a particularly good speaker, so I didn't know how to talk to camera. And my English was not great then, because for the previous couple of years I had spent so much time being in Korea and hanging mostly around Korean people in Australia that I hadn't been speaking in English that much. So I sounded like

I'd just arrived. If you don't speak a language for a long time you lose a lot of it. It can come back if you start speaking again, but at that stage I hadn't spoken English much at all for months.

When it was time for me to audition, around midnight, I was nervous – as I had been all day – and really tired. I waited around for so long and I could vaguely see the performers going on before me. I could see the judges making comments even though I couldn't hear what they were saying. I remember thinking, *Those judges must be so tired! They've been doing that all day.* And not just that day: they would've done it the day before and the day before that. *What a tough job.*

To be honest, I was quite cynical about the whole TV show process because I knew that a lot of what the show was about was to entertain people and create something dramatic. I was a part of the show as a contestant who needed to impress the judges and get through, but I was also an observer on how a reality TV show gets made. When I went onto that stage and started singing, the judges looked gobsmacked and surprised. One by one, all four judges stood and gave me a standing ovation.

Some people would organically react to what was going on whereas I felt like I was outside of my body as an observer. It made me giggle inside that they were giving me such a huge reaction and showing that through their bodies with big gestures. Even after such a long day of watching hundreds of performances, they gave me a dramatic standing ovation.

I was also confused about what was happening before I sang, when the judges were asking me questions – because the producers had asked me really similar questions backstage. I was standing there wondering, *Am I meant to answer it the same way? Am I meant to say something a bit different?* All while being filmed for national television for the first time. As you might imagine, there was a lot going on so I was confused and constantly overthinking!

However, despite being quite cynical at the time I was ecstatic that I'd made it through. While also thinking that the judges were very good at their jobs and that I wasn't going to get too sucked into the whole machine where my emotions would be out of control because of what happened.

I was aware that even though I'd made it through that audition, the producers might decide to edit me out – which would mean I wouldn't end up in the show at all, regardless of what happened during the audition. I just kept telling myself that if they decided I wasn't interesting enough and they edited me out, I might not even end up on air. And even if I was on air I didn't know how long I would last on the show.

In other words, my expectations were very low going in. And my goal at the time was to perform on TV at least once so that I could get some exposure and be able to get more gigs and opportunities to perform in Australia, because that was the reason I went on the show.

Still, after it was over I thought, *I got a standing ovation from all four judges, so there's a good chance they'll show me on TV.* That was the exciting part, not the ovation itself. I certainly didn't think, *Full standing ovation – I must be amazing!* That might have been the reaction of a fourteen-year-old, but I was a little more muted. And I didn't think any of it was life-changing.

As we know now, I was shown on air and I did make it through to the next round – but no further at that time because I was not selected as one of the top twenty-four, due to the fact that I fluffed my performance of 'Jolene' in the second round. It wasn't a song I was familiar with because I hadn't grown up with a lot of American pop/country music, and it's quite a challenging song to sing even if you know it well. Which I didn't. So I forgot some of the words, mucked up the song, and that was the end of it.

Or so I thought.

The way I made it back into *The X Factor* after that is quite a story, so bear with me. The categories on the show included: girls aged twenty-four and under, boys aged twenty-four and under, and both men and women aged over twenty-five. The fourth category was for groups: trios, girl groups, boy bands, whatever. I was twenty-four at the time, so that put me in the first category.

Just before they gave the verdict of who was getting through to the top twenty-four, they suddenly picked me and two guys to tell us that they'd changed the categories. The new categorisation was twenty-four and over rather than twenty-five and over, so now I was in the overs, which contained both men and women, and that changed who I was competing against for slots.

Then when they announced the verdict, I found out I wasn't getting through. And the reason was that they put this other guy through – who was also twenty-four. Obviously there hadn't been enough room to fit him in the boys' twenty-four and under group, so they'd changed the classifications.

So then it was all over. I went home; it was all really depressing. Noah was sick at the time – he was in hospital. Everything was dismal. I wasn't getting any more phone calls, there were no more emails. It was just really *over*. And it all stopped so quickly, which felt like a shock after so much activity.

Up until that point we'd gone through an incredibly intense process as well. We were staying at The Star

Hotel for almost a week, which actually felt like months of my life, as every single day we were rehearsing, filming, performing with really long days, and going through that was exhausting. There were a lot of ups and downs, and a lot of waiting around again.

Those emotional roller-coasters were not like anything else I'd experienced before. It was so exciting one minute and then it was so disappointing. Forgetting the words to the song then the verdict all happened within a forty-five-minute segment on television, but it took a few days – the tension was long and drawn out as the contestants waited to find out if we'd made it through. So to have that intensity and be communicating with the producers for so long, even before being there physically – all the organisation – then coming home afterwards to nothing was hard to adjust to. All the adrenaline I'd produced during that week on the show had to go somewhere and it was a deflating experience.

Obviously the producers couldn't look after the thousands of people who didn't get through that very first round but once we got through to the TV auditions it was a smaller group and the stakes were different. The hardest thing was probably having that silence where before there had been so much activity. This really exciting door was open for weeks and months, ever since the audition, then it was shut in a moment, abruptly in front of my face. Even though I'd gone into *The X Factor* with low expectations, I really hadn't expected that.

With the benefit of more experience I can now say that feeling was similar to what musicians or performers experience after they've finished a tour. There's all this craziness on the road then you're back home to your normal life and thinking, *What do I do with my life?* So what happened to me on the show was actually a taste of what lay ahead of me as a performing artist.

A few weeks after I was sent home, one of Mum's church friends who believes in the more supernatural way God works told Mum, 'I can feel that something's coming for Dami. Something is happening.' I was fairly sceptical about it, but it was kind of her to think of me.

Then one day as I was driving out of a Westfield car park, I got a call from an unknown number. It was one of the producers saying, 'Someone had to pull out and we might have a place for you as a back-up to fill that spot.'

I was pretty stunned.

'Are you up for it?' they asked.

And my reply was, 'I'm *so* up for it!'

I found out later that they went to someone else and asked him to come back, but he didn't want to do it. So I wasn't even their first choice to return! But as a second choice my response was, 'Take me now!'

So I was back in the game in the over-twenty-four category. And if it hadn't been for this guy that they'd switched the teams around for, I wouldn't even have been able to go back because there wouldn't have been room for me. They'd have had to get somebody else.

Once I was back on the show the first thing they did was fly me to New York, because that's where everyone in my category went. Some of the others went to Los Angeles, some to London, and some to Queensland – luckily for me that wasn't my group!

Dannii Minogue was the mentor in my category so she came with us to New York. Being in that city was such a great experience.

Because Dannii was our mentor, her sister, Kylie, became involved. When I was at school Kylie was somebody all my friends were obsessed with. Growing up, she was a cultural icon especially for us girls. So when I saw her in person I couldn't help thinking, *I can't wait till this goes to air and all my friends see it!*

New York is such a breathtaking city. A city that is so vibrant and full of people, buildings and traffic, hustling and bustling. I had been to New York before but this time everything seemed even more electric in my mind. It was a short trip, only about four days long, and a lot was packed into it. We were put up in a small but beautiful boutique hotel and we filmed from morning till night. It was surreal being back on the show after everything that had happened, and this time I was determined to give it my best shot.

In the first few rounds, I had been keeping an emotional distance partly because I was cynical about reality TV shows, but it was also about not letting myself be disappointed. I was only half-committed knowing that I could be kicked out at any minute. I was holding back as I felt uncomfortable that my fate was out of my hands. But this time was different. I knew not to take this opportunity for granted. I really wanted to stay and get chosen for the next round. I wanted to be in the Top Twelve live shows and I was going to do everything I could to make that happen.

When I made it through to the Top Twelve I was ecstatic. It really felt like God had led me to this point through all the unlikely circumstances lining up to make it that way. From that point on it was going to be on a completely different level from the previous rounds. The Top Twelve would go live on air every Sunday and Monday. We were all going to be living in Sydney at accommodation they put us up in, and we wouldn't get to go home until we were eliminated. The decisions were made 100 per cent by the audience vote. It wasn't the judges or the producers anymore. One contestant would be eliminated each week because of that vote.

Up until that point, we had all dressed ourselves and put on our own make-up and decided which songs we wanted to sing. We'd discuss it with the producers and they had a say, but we could still choose.

From the time I was in the Top Twelve live rounds, though, I had access to incredible resources. For the first time I was working with a whole team of people who were experts in their fields, luxuries I hadn't had before because singing in a church or a little bar, there's no stagecraft, there are no costumes. But on the show I was working with top-of-their-game stylists, make-up artists, music producers, choreographers and set designers.

The staging and the costumes and props and dancers and all those things would come together to form a world within the couple of minutes that each performance lasted, and to be at the centre of that was incredible.

I knew my limits, and how to stage a musical number wasn't something I was used to doing, so I was excited to work with these teams. Obviously I got to have a say – if I didn't feel comfortable with something it would be altered. But I also loved being able to trust them and seeing these professionals bring their ideas, put them together and bring them to life was extraordinary.

The stylist was a woman named Heather and I would continue to work with her for years afterwards, until she moved to Los Angeles. It was amazing to see what she and the other behind-the-scenes people could do. Admittedly, sometimes I look back and think, *That didn't age very well.* Even at the time, some of the make-up and costumes were a bit much compared with what I was used to and I wouldn't repeat them if I had the chance. The lizard wings attached to my arms that I got to spread wide, along with the heavy black eyeshadow that made me look like my eyes were open even when they were closed, for example. But there were plenty of looks that I think are still quite impressive today.

What we were pulling together each time was really experimental. I love being able to take an audience to another world through my performance, and all the sets and costumes helped me do that, because it's not just about the singing and the song: there's this dimension to performance and on *The X Factor* that was really powerful.

While I embraced all those other parts of performing, and enjoyed the process of transforming each week, I did occasionally have to make little adjustments. The stylist obviously always wants the performer to look amazing – but they don't always think about the functionality.

'I'm so sorry,' I would say, 'but I've got to be able to breathe!'

I hesitated to say anything at first, as the styling team was so passionate about putting a look together, like they were building a sculpture. I had dresses custom made by Australia's leading couture designers such as J'Aton, who made the dress I wore for the performance of 'And I Am Telling You I'm Not Going' in the final, and George Elsissa, who created my dress for the winning performance of 'Alive'. But I figured if I can't sing because of how good the waistline was going to look, it just wasn't going to work. I knew that this might mean the look wouldn't be as striking as the stylist originally conceived, but I had to make the call to get an outfit altered if it was going to hinder a performance in any way.

Some of the other contestants were really nervous about letting the people do their jobs and very protective of how they were going to be portrayed. But I was open to their ideas and my attitude was, 'I'll try anything' – provided I could still sing! I could see the producers and the rest of the team having fun being able to do that with me. They were all creative people, and I tend to find that when creative people are given the opportunity to do whatever they want, they bring the best to the table.

As a performer, when you let other professionals do their jobs it can also take some pressure off you – they're helping you put on the best performance possible rather than you trying to figure it all out yourself. The result in my case was that the studio audience and the public really liked my performances and they showed it by voting for me. The looks that we were able to create as a team were striking and avant-garde, sometimes a bit outrageous, which I believe is crucial for the stage. In the end I believe I got some of the best staging and costumes out of all of the contestants and that, no doubt, helped with the result.

I'm so glad I approached the show with that attitude. After the show, for years, I continued to figure out who I am as an artist. Sometimes that meant choosing crazy costumes, as I'd had on the show; sometimes not.

It was a process of finding what fits me and something that lets me create interesting work but still stay true to who I am as an artist and as a person. I come from a very stripped-back performance style which focused on the message in the song. *The X Factor* was a going-all-out experience and it was a good lesson in seeing how far I could take that, to the extreme.

The X Factor enabled me to bring together everything I had learned by that point. Those experiences playing to five grandmas in a rural church in Korea, when I'd adapted my set list to suit the audience, when I'd figured out a way to work with the equipment at hand, prepared me to come into a situation that was completely beyond what I knew. I was used to that, and I was also used to feeling that I didn't have a choice but to adapt and make it work because I was already there and I wanted to put on the best show I could.

In essence what I did in all of those situations was just try to be able to work and find my laneway as an artist. Being an unknown Christian singer, you do whatever you can to adapt and you sing what they want you to sing, basically. And even on *The X Factor* I had to have the same attitude. I'm not used to doing this and I have the opportunity to work with experts who have done this for a lot longer than me, so I'm just going to roll with it. Before you can say no, it's important that you experience things and see how they turn out – because it could have been a yes, I just might not have known if I didn't try.

The live television shows went for ten weeks or so. My first live performance was of 'One' by U2. It's a very famous song but I'd never heard it because that wasn't the sort of music I'd been listening to. I loved that performance, though, partly because I got to play the piano and that's where I feel the most comfortable. Well, it wasn't entirely comfortable, as this piano was hung in the air. It was easily my most dramatic entry ever!

The workload of *The X Factor* was intense. As I mentioned, the live shows took place every Sunday and Monday – that is, live in studio and live-to-air on television. That meant everything had to be rehearsed – the individual songs, and the shows as a whole – and there was very little time from week to week.

I was given a new song on the Tuesday of each week and I had to learn it, work on the craft, work on the staging and the performance and get that memorised by Thursday when we had to rehearse on stage. By Friday we were doing the full dress rehearsals.

Each Tuesday, when I was given the song, I had to work out an arrangement with the musical director because we weren't singing straight covers of these songs – we were trying to make our own versions of them and create suitable arrangements for the competition. Then we were learning that different version.

The time on the show was a big learning curve for me, in music and in performance. My vocals improved a lot in those weeks because I had never practised that much in my life. Our vocal coach, Gary Pinto, was with us from early on in the show throughout the whole process. He was amazing – so intuitively musical – and would help us with the vocal arrangements. He was a man of faith who was a great support to the contestants as well, because there were a few tears along the way due to the stress levels.

There were group songs that we had to learn too, and some weeks there were two of those. Essentially we had two days to learn new songs and make sure they were good enough to be performed live.

Two days may be okay if you're already familiar with the material but I hadn't even heard of a lot of the songs we were given. They might have been familiar to the other contestants, because they were popular songs, but I didn't know most of them because I hadn't grown up with that music.

So I was learning a lot of songs from scratch – which was what happened with 'Jolene'. After having forgotten the words to that song, I wasn't going to make the same mistake again. You can mess up once, but the public's not going to forgive you for forgetting words again. So that was extra pressure because I always find learning and memorising lyrics really hard. Trying to perfect a song – with no mistakes in the lyrics – in two days was the hardest part. The possibility of forgetting a line was terrifying for me, so I would practise in the apartment where we were living.

In between practice and rehearsals we had to do all these interviews, including breakfast radio interviews, and there were also some other filming commitments: social media content and commercials.

All the while the contestants were living together in Sydney. So I didn't go home for months. And some days

I was so tired I didn't even have the time or energy to eat, all I wanted to do was collapse into bed.

There were a few clear favourites among the contestants and I wasn't one of them; everyone else was getting a lot more screen time. But after that dramatic first performance of 'One', I started getting attention and phone calls, and the producers knew that I was the public's favourite.

On that first day I performed on the live shows, I overheard the producers talking to each other. 'Hey, so the commercials are going to be about Dami,' said one.

That's when I started to get interviews from the producers and the cameras started to follow me around, whereas before I'd been in the dark most of the time while other people were getting interviewed.

The second week was an important week. It was the week I performed 'Purple Rain' and many of my fans remember me from that time, and that's the performance they mention the most. I still sing that song in a lot of my shows because it was the highlight of my *X Factor* journey.

The producers put me on last that week and that order means something on a television show – the performer on last is the one people are looking forward to the most. Whether you're going to do well that week or not is a different matter! But the order means people will tune in and not turn the TV off until you've been on.

So I was on last with 'Purple Rain' and, again, I didn't know the song before it was given to me on the Tuesday. I just belted it out. I felt something transition while we were workshopping it – I figured out how I was going to sing it and what the arrangement would be.

I could belt out songs before that, but I didn't because I didn't think it was necessary. I had been restraining myself because it didn't feel super necessary to use my full range, but it was clear that's what people got excited about. I didn't have to belt throughout the whole thing, but for certain moments it was like a weapon that I hadn't used before and then suddenly I realised, *Okay, I should go there.*

The studio gave me a full standing ovation for that song and I realised that people really responded to the full range in my voice. That's when I became aware that I have a powerful voice, and a big one. I didn't think of myself as that kind of singer until that point, and I'd been singing different types of music – lighter songs and jazz.

Throughout *The X Factor*, singing powerfully became my thing. Week to week, after that, I was never in the bottom two who had to battle it out.

My parents flew in from Brisbane each week to watch me. My cynicism comes from Dad and he's a little bit pessimistic in some ways – or a realist, whichever way you want to look at it. So every single week of *The X Factor* he would say, 'This could be my daughter's last week.' That's why they only booked flights one week at a time. Which is fair enough. But it was also funny because I was getting standing ovation after standing ovation each week and was never in the bottom two, so the odds seemed good that I'd go a fair way into the competition.

While my parents were feeling cautious, I was enjoying myself. I got to dress up in all these different costumes. For Disco Week I wore a bumblebee outfit with a big hooded cape and sang Thelma Houston's 'Don't Leave Me This Way'. There was a beautiful heartfelt 'Bridge Over Troubled Waters' moment with a lovely organza dress that looked like a tutu. And that was the one song I actually knew because my parents liked it and I used to sing it.

Each week was really different and while it was hard work I enjoyed it and learned so much. I could feel myself exploring and growing. Everything was fresh and because I didn't have a preconceived idea about what was going to happen, I was open to new experiences. Each week I wouldn't know that the songs I was given were known to most people and that the audience would have a connection to them. So I wanted to do well, but I always wanted to make the song my own, and not knowing them freed me in some ways. Making them my own was my biggest focus and priority because I thought, *Well, if these are big, well-known songs, what's the point of doing them again if I'm not going to bring something different?* And with the staging and the designs, it was fun trying to create a different world each week. Each week I'd wonder, *What else can I do?*

One week was Rock Week and I sang a Foo Fighters song wearing a bejewelled see-through outfit with gold fringe hanging off me – nothing like I had ever worn before on- or offstage. That was part of my process: wondering how far I could push myself into different genres and different types of performances. *When else am I going to be doing such crazy performances?* I'd say to myself each time. If it was a normal show I probably would have had to stick to some kind of genre and pattern and there wouldn't have been the chance to explore different types of music, but *The X Factor* was an amazing opportunity to go all-out, and to have fun. And so I did.

It's possible that having fun was part of the reason I had so much success on the show – if I was having fun I was relaxed, I wasn't trying to control everything that happened and worrying if I couldn't, and that translated to my performances. I remember some other contestants feeling uptight about what song they had to sing and what outfit they were given, whereas I enjoyed the craziness of it all – as long as I could sing my best and I wasn't forgetting the words and I was interpreting the song the way I wanted to. It meant I could make decisions about what was best for the song as well as for me, because I was motivated to have fun rather than winning being my sole focus.

I did have one bad week, when I sang John Farnham's 'You're the Voice'. I knew it wasn't just a famous song – it's an Australian anthem, pretty much. But I wanted to make it different and I think I tried too hard, so it just ended up becoming a mess and the judges' comments reflected that.

But I think I needed to have a bad week – in terms of how the show worked – because otherwise it would have been eight consecutive weeks of standing ovations and praise. I knew something was coming. I didn't plan to have a bad week but it ended up being the perfect moment to have one. It gave me another push from my fans because they didn't want me to be voted off.

Actually, that's when the term 'Dami Army' started because some people began to refer to my supporters by that name. So many of my fans have supported me since then and the Dami Army is still going strong. So much of my strength and success comes from the support of the Dami Army and how much passion they have in following my journey.

Despite the slip-up on 'You're the Voice', after seven weeks of standing ovations and praise from the judges, plus never being in the bottom two, I could see the possibility of winning the competition, but I was never sure and I didn't want to get my hopes up, because I didn't want to be disappointed.

Being on a TV show like *The X Factor* means, to an extent, becoming a character. In those forty-five minutes of television in each episode, they can't possibly show who each contestant is. But they did do a relatively good job at painting what kind of person each contestant was. They didn't make up someone who didn't exist. The show highlighted the real nature of each person, but we were condensed into a simplified caricature. I felt that only one side of me was exaggerated.

What was strange and new for me was that all of a sudden everybody seemed to think that they knew me and they would treat me a certain way. And I definitely felt very one-dimensional when people expected things from me.

One thing that was difficult was when everyone kept asking me when I was having a baby. And this was during the height of the show, when I was clearly occupied with that! The contestants had to do media in between episodes, and I didn't know anything about the nature of media and how I should talk to them. So one journalist asked about my plans to have babies and I said, 'I don't really have a plan because obviously I'm on *The X Factor*.' I was doing all this hard work, living away from home for months. Clearly babies were not on the cards. And then they asked me if I would have babies one day and I said, 'Yeah, probably.'

'Do you think they'll play music?' was the next question.

'I suppose they will because I play music,' I replied, cringeing.

What ended up on the cover of *New Idea* was the headline 'X Factor Dami: My Baby News!' The article said that I would have babies who would play music and how I couldn't wait. I was naive enough to give them what they needed to be able to write that headline – but I know better now.

From then on I kept getting asked in interviews – and by strangers on the street – if I was pregnant. When would I be having these babies? People were focused on me having babies.

For me, this was the most awful part of the whole experience.

I think every woman has a different relationship to this kind of thing and some people might have found it funny or just brushed it off. But I was already so afraid of this happening to me with marriage and having kids.

I was terrified of people associating me with babies as if that was the only thing I could do in my life. And now the whole world was associating me with babies.

Whenever they'd see me in a dress that showed some kind of a belly – because I was eating, usually – the headlines would be 'pregnancy, pregnancy'.

I actually found it really offensive at the time because they seemed to think that just because I was married I was only good for having kids, when I was a professional musician working full-time on a television show. Did they think I was doing all of that just so I could go home and have kids? It was completely disrespectful. What about my talent and this being something that I'd worked towards my whole life? It seemed that they were intent on defining me as a mother and nothing else; the message seemed to be that I had no business being on the show, that I should be at home looking after children.

I am completely conscious of the fact that some people really want to be mothers and that's their dream – even still, they are people too, they don't exist just to be mothers. And especially at that time, there were other things I wanted to do. Those things included being on *The X Factor* and that line of questioning from journalists diminished that as well, treating it as if it was a placeholder activity for me when it was pretty much my sole focus.

There is no way to prepare for something like that – for your body and your life to be commented on by strangers just because you're doing a particular job. It wasn't as if the producers of *The X Factor* sat us down and said we'd be appearing in magazines and that those magazines could say whatever they liked. I hadn't been on television before; I didn't have a burning desire to be famous. I went on the show because I wanted to work more as a singer. Now there were these other elements to deal with that were so strange and out of the realm of my experience.

So I became frustrated with this public image and persona. And when it came to babies I was the opposite of what they thought this character was. So that was tricky to navigate at the start.

I did consider that maybe the way I was presented in the media was because there was a perception of me as a nice married Christian girl with a lovely husband. I wondered if it would have been different if I was a badass rock star or something. And I just kept thinking, *Do I look like a mum?*

I didn't address it at the time, though. I didn't say anything for seven years because I knew if I talked about it, I would be associated with pregnancy. It was hard to not say anything because it put me in a loop: people would keep asking if I didn't address it, but if

I said anything some people would misinterpret it and would assume I was pregnant. I felt so trapped in that little annoying pregnancy thing while also finding it very weird that there was so much interest in that subject.

Those years after *The X Factor* were definitely years of experimenting and learning, and without having done that I wouldn't have got to a place where I felt I knew who I was as an artist. Maybe it was being open minded that helped me get to where I got to in the end.

* * *

By the night of the grand final I was exhausted. There had been a lot of commitments for all of the contestants throughout the show. The ratings were so high back then, in the days before streaming entertainment – millions of people tuned into the final – and our show got so much attention from all over the country. We had to do all these interviews, photoshoots and video shoots in between these performances and twice-weekly shows. Plus I'd lost quite a bit of weight by then, by just naturally being so busy and tired.

I'd been away from home for many months and I was so ready to be back in Brisbane. But I was glad I'd made it that far. It felt like it was this very moment that we'd all been working towards in our careers – certainly in mine. I couldn't believe that I had ended up in the top three and that I was in the final.

On the night itself I was nervous, but in a different way – not just for my performance, because each time I performed I would worry about making mistakes on live television. On the final night, though, I also had to think about what was going to happen at the end of the show: someone would be announced the winner. It was really scary. *What happens if I win?* I knew I had a good chance of winning but, as ever, I wasn't sure. It was something I needed to contemplate, though, and I became quite nervous and anxious about what winning would mean and how it would affect my life. Which was, fundamentally, fear of the unknown, which we all have.

I remember sitting backstage that night and talking to everyone, saying, 'I don't know if I want to win because I don't know what that means. I don't know how that would change my life.' The other contestants would've been so frustrated that I would even say things like that because they just wanted to win. And obviously I did too, but also I was hesitant in some ways. I was overthinking everything and I always had this question: *If I win, is that a good thing? Because that means somebody else loses and other people become jealous.* All these thoughts. *How will this change my life? Will it be a good thing for me?* So it wasn't just as simple as, *I'll try to win.*

Maybe that was the practical thing to do, to think about what would happen if I won – the pros and the cons – because that's how I could make the most of it if it happened. If I'd only been focused on winning itself, and if I'd believed that winning would change my life only in positive ways, I might not have known what to do afterwards. It was also, I suppose, the scepticism that I learned from Dad that kept me in a mindset of thinking that the whole situation was a bit weird and I shouldn't place too many hopes and dreams into it. Because a big part of what was weird about it was that it was happening live. It wasn't as if the final was recorded months before it was broadcast, as happens often nowadays with those sorts of shows. I would find out the result along with everyone else and therefore if I won I would have very little time to prepare for what came next. So in my own way I was planning ahead.

There were aspects to being on the show that I'd already had to adjust to – for example, I'd started to be recognised whenever I went to the shops to get lunch or whatever. Fame wasn't something I'd aspired to but now I seemed to be somewhat famous and that was very different from what I knew of life before. I know I'm not the first person to find it hard to be recognised.

It wasn't a case of, *Oh my gosh, I'm famous. How exciting is that?* It was more, *Oh, people keep coming up to me and talking to me,* and I didn't know how to handle all that. So that was part of the reason why I was questioning the value of winning: *Do I even want this to keep happening to me?* There was a lot of pressure that came with being famous.

I never did *The X Factor* so I could win and become a celebrity. I did it because I wanted to have more opportunities to perform. That was my aim, but then suddenly I was a celebrity and famous. I not only questioned whether I actually wanted that, but also why it was being given to me and what I should do with it. I was just there to do my best each week. I tried to find meaning in each song and I took it week by week. The other parts of it happened *to* me and weren't anything I had control over.

I found being famous very difficult for quite some time. It can feel lonely because no-one else actually understands – except maybe your family – that it's not awesome to be recognised. Everyone else thinks you should be grateful, but I didn't actually sign up for that part of it. It was a by-product of signing up to sing. People wanted to have photos taken with me every single day. If anyone stopped to think about that, it's a really odd circumstance to have strangers approaching you as if you're their friend and asking to have a photo taken with you. For someone as introverted as me, it was quite a struggle.

Part of why performers like me can end up in that position is, possibly, because the people involved in creating the show haven't ever been through the process themselves – they've never found themselves suddenly famous, so they don't know how it feels and, therefore, they don't know how to support anyone who is going through it. Because it is a process that changes everything – my old life was gone and I hadn't even had a chance to say goodbye to it. That is not to say that I didn't appreciate all the support from the public, because I absolutely did. It's more to say that I wish I'd been better prepared for the huge changes the show would bring to my life.

I have moments that I'm really ashamed of when I didn't respond well to someone who approached me. I had some pretty bad days – I still do sometimes – and I'd have been crying all day. Noah would take me out for a walk and someone would come and want photos with me. Sometimes I pretended not to be me and I kept going, and I knew they knew it was me. That was embarrassing. But some days it was really hard to handle.

I think it's also because I don't have that extrovert quality. These days I'm much better with it because I know it's part of my job. I've accepted that. But back then, I struggled talking to strangers. I barely talked to my friends, and I had to be an outgoing celebrity and it was exhausting at a time when I was already so worn out with all the things being thrown at me. Speaking to strangers was another level of energy I didn't have in that period. But now I can look back and see clearly what was going on, and I apologise to anybody I was not nice to during that time.

Perhaps part of why I found it hard to manage that side of things was that I had never planned to be on television; I had never sought an audience beyond anyone who was in a venue where I was playing. So I was questioning everything about my place on the show. But I can say now that I am still amazed by the process of it all, even this many years later, because I know the producers couldn't have planned what happened, with me going home from the show then being brought back in. They planned something else and that didn't work out. So I ended up having this incredible life-changing opportunity. And I'm also amazed by what happened to me after the show finished. I wasn't so cynical about that because by then I really felt like the whole thing was God's plan and it was meant to be like this, it wasn't some human saying, 'Oh yeah, we'll just pick her.'

I do believe that God led me through that whole process. I just wasn't spiritually sensitive – I think that's the way to say it. At my church some people would have visions and hear voices, they'd feel supernatural things. Whereas even though I grew up in the same church and went to the same services, I didn't tend to experience those things. I think I'm wired a bit differently to that. A bit more cognitive and analytical.

That doesn't mean I don't believe in the supernatural – just that my body doesn't pick things up like that. When I was a teenager I struggled with it actually, because it seemed like everybody was experiencing all these things, seeing things and dreaming things, whereas I was ... normal. It's just the way I am.

Having said that, I did feel like there was an invisible hand guiding me through the whole process. When I was sent home after that second round, it was over as far as I was concerned. I could never have hoped that they'd call me back and I was only brought back because there was a problem. It wasn't like I was a wild card who the producers wanted to reintroduce for ratings. It wasn't a programming decision made to get more viewers. They had a person pull out so they needed to fill a gap; then they couldn't get their first choice so they got their second choice. And I was that second choice. So it did feel like fate. And it changed my life.

Meeting Dannii Minogue and having her as my mentor on the show was such a blessing as well. She was so genuine and caring throughout. On our rare days off, she would invite me to her house in Sydney and we'd spend the afternoon together on the beach and have lunch together. Even after the show was over, we were keeping in touch and she was involved in making sure that I was being looked after. I genuinely learned a lot from working with her and I will always count myself lucky for that.

Clockwise from top left:
Grandfather sitting in
his orchard dressed in
his *hanbok*; Mum and
Dad with me as a baby;
with Kenny outside our
Runcorn house;
with my family on my
birthday at the Runcorn
house; and my parents
as newlyweds – Dad
loved playing his guitar.

Clockwise from above: When we went back to Korea for end-of-year holidays for Christmas and New Year's, we took our instruments with us to jam with our relatives at Grandma's house; playing piano at the school chapel, not long after we arrived in Australia; performing at Brisbane's Queen Street Mall after joining the Young Conservatorium in 1999; and playing the flute at school.

Far left: Singing at a Korean church in Cairns. The white fabric is covering the communion table, not a dead body! *Left*: my first televised audition on *The X Factor* in 2013.

The amped-up version of my 'Purple Rain' performance in the *X Factor* finals, with water falling from above.

Far left: Having lunch at Dannii Minogue's. *Left*: Running into Dannii at the Channel 10 studios. Seeing her always makes me so happy!

Clockwise from above:
Performing 'Sound of
Silence' at the Eurovision
Grand Final; Noah and I
feeling ecstatic as we were
given twelve points by
another country; and singing
into my lemonade at the
afterparty drinks, straight
after the Grand Final.

Meeting my sponsor child Jovia (*left*) in Uganda in 2016, a few weeks after Eurovision. We spent quite a few days playing with the children in the village. Even though the conditions were tough, they were full of laughter and light.

Clockwise from above left: During filming of *Dancing with the Stars*, with Celia Pacquola, Ed Kavalee, Beau Ryan and Travis Cloke; backstage at *MasterChef*, with Rebecca Gibney and Ian Thorpe; performing at the Prime Minister's Olympic Dinner in 2016 with Russell Morris and John Farnham; and with Olivia Newton-John when I performed for one of her fundraisers.

Top: Having the best time touring and performing for my fans. *Middle*: I went over to Nashville to work with producer Rick Price on my fourth album. He was so great to work with, and Noah joined me for a few days to enjoy the musical city. *Left*: Performing with opera singer Sumi Jo was a moment that my family was very proud of.

Clockwise from above: The traditional ceremony for our wedding in 2012; our official white wedding photo; with Harry at two weeks old; and performing at Byron Bay Bluesfest while thirty-seven weeks pregnant.

CHAPTER NINE

A New World

*I*t's hard to describe what it was like in the days after *The X Factor* ended – not because I don't remember but because it was such an unusual experience. How could I explain it to anyone else? Even the people closest to me didn't have the same experience I did. Something truly life-changing had happened *to me* and there was really no-one else I knew who could relate.

I'd gone into a competition, just as I had with all those eisteddfods, and I'd won, but on television in front of millions of people and suddenly I had fans and a record deal and strangers approaching me on the street. There were days when it felt like it might be happening to someone else – except it was very definitely happening to me.

After the show finished we all went to the after-party. The whole crew and the cast who had been working on this for months and months were letting their hair down, dancing and drinking and talking – but I only stayed until just past 1 am. I had to be there because I was the winner, although I left early because the next morning my media commitments began, and the first was a performance on *Sunrise*, Channel Seven's breakfast show.

I had less than three hours' sleep as I had to be up at 4 am to have make-up and hair done so I could be on *Sunrise* between 6 am and 7 am. It was the start of a massive run of interviews – that day I did eighty across TV, radio and print. So that's basically talking about the same thing eighty times and trying to make it sound interesting each time – not something I could rehearse! I did my best and I don't know if I sounded bored by the end of it; I certainly couldn't remember if I had said something before or if I'd said it in another interview.

In between the interviews I had a meeting so I could be introduced to people from Sony, which was now the record company where I was a signed artist. One by one, all these new faces came and introduced themselves to me – telling me their name and what their job title was, but I didn't remember or understand any of it. This was a completely new world.

On the back of all that I had to fly to Melbourne to finish recording my album. The tracks on the album were longer versions of the top twelve songs that I'd performed on *The X Factor*, so at least I knew them and didn't have to go into the process cold, because there wasn't much time to record – we only had a few days. It could be completed in that short time frame because they already had arrangements done. The recordings would be essentially the same versions of those songs I'd performed on *The X Factor* but extended so they could be full songs, whereas the live performances were only about half the length.

I wasn't daunted by the experience because I was used to recording to a studio microphone, which is a different skill to singing live or performing in general. It also didn't take me long to learn the rest of the songs and sing them – all those years of having to learn pieces of music for competitions paid off. And I actually enjoyed the recording process. That was the good part. Amid the whirlwind of signings and strangers, being in the soundproofed studio just focusing on singing these songs was like being in my little oasis. I spent a few days in Melbourne recording at the iconic Sing Sing Studios with producer Dorian West. I thought, *Yes, this is what I always wanted to do!*

Usually it takes months to record, mix and master an album, and have it ready for release. There was no such luxury of time with this record, because Sony wanted it out as quickly as possible, to make the most of the attention that had been on the show. The time from recording to release – including the pressing of CDs, as this was in the days before streaming – was about a fortnight.

Once the album was released I did in-store appearances at shopping centres combined with media in all these different cities. I didn't have to do quite as many as eighty interviews in a day again but there were still massive media days and photoshoots, and everywhere I was going for an in-store there was press to go along with it. I could be doing a photoshoot in a rural area in the morning then dashing off to the city for an in-store in the afternoon. That was my life for a month or two after the show finished.

There were big queues at the in-stores; people would come up to have an album signed and tell me how much they enjoyed the show and how they voted for me. They were tiring but it was also kind of fun because I could actually see people who had watched the show. The times when I found it tough to have people coming up to me were when I was in the middle of doing something else – such as being on a call for an interview, or rushing off to catch a plane – but at an in-store I was there to see my fans. That didn't mean it didn't wear me out! I hadn't done something like that before so I didn't know how relentless it could be, signing and talking for so long. In the final analysis, though, it was quite special to actually meet the fans in real life.

The record and the single released just after the finale of *The X Factor* both went to number one everywhere. And, looking back, I know I took that for granted. I wasn't thinking, *Oh my gosh, that's amazing. My dream's been achieved!* I actually felt quite indifferent. A little too numb. Now I realise how hard it is to get a good chart position, let alone being number one on the ARIA chart. I understand now just how much work it takes combined with incredible amounts of luck and perfect timing for someone to achieve this kind of result. Now, like most artists, I would kill to be able to do that, but back then I didn't realise this.

Partly I was blasé about it because I was only half-involved – there was the TV show and the record company and the ratings that pumped this train full-steam that I felt like I just happened to jump on. Of course I was part of the mix, but it didn't feel completely like *my* success.

Around this time the top six contestants from the show went on an *X Factor* tour – rehearsing and touring was fitted in around media for the album and interviews. The hectic days of working on the show probably prepared me for all of this to an extent, but at times it did feel like I didn't know which day of the week it was, even as I was so grateful for the opportunity I was being given.

Before *The X Factor* I had played shows of all kinds – but I had never played at a corporate function. That quickly changed, as I was booked in for many corporate gigs by my new manager, who was part of the deal for the winner. I didn't know it at the time but his management company was part-owned by Sony, my new record company, and I also didn't know that these corporate gigs were a big money-maker for management, as they took a commission on every show I played.

Back in those days I was ruled by schedules I never actually got to see. I was meant to be sent details of the weeks ahead so I would know where I'd have to be and when, and what I'd have to do – perform, be interviewed, do a photoshoot – but instead I was just told the day before, or the morning of, which city I was flying to and what I was doing. I should have demanded more details, I suppose, but this was also my first time doing anything like this and I didn't know what to expect. I didn't want to be seen as demanding.

But try to imagine not knowing what you are doing tomorrow or the day after, and there's no way of knowing when that state will end. After a life of making decisions for myself, it was a strange and hard adjustment. On top of that, each day was crammed full of commitments and I was exhausted. All I wanted to do was go home. It would be an understatement to say I was not enjoying life at that stage. If I'd had expectations of what winning would be like I would have been disappointed; luckily, I'd had no expectations – I was just tired and homesick.

Part of the challenge for me during those weeks was that I couldn't plan ahead, which meant I couldn't mentally prepare for anything. Even if you have a crazy week, if you are prepared mentally you can manage it, but, as I mentioned, I didn't know what was coming until they told me the day before or the day of. It was pretty disorganised and it also left me feeling like I was being something I don't ever want to be: unprofessional.

It was during the tour with the other contestants that it all started to catch up to me. During the shows I had to sing the most number of songs out of everyone, because I was the winner of the show. I sang seven songs back-to-back, and they were all songs I'd performed on the TV show – and they all had incredibly high notes. They weren't easy to sing – in fact, each of them was high in intensity and really challenging.

I became sick at one point halfway through the tour and lost my voice. That meant there was no more singing. That's the point at which everything became really stressful, because I was still doing in-stores while the tour was on.

I wanted to try to see if I could cancel one of the in-stores – it was to take place between two of the shows and I had no voice, so I wouldn't be able to talk to people who came to have a CD signed.

Ken Outch, the marketing manager from Sony who was working on promoting my album, called Denis Handlin, the boss of Sony, to tell him that I was sick that morning and ask if it was possible for me to cancel the in-store so I could improve my chances of being able to sing in the shows.

Denis's response was, 'If Delta [Goodrem] can sign while having cancer, Dami can sign with a cold.'

I thought the in-store was cancelled so in the morning I jumped in the car to get to the airport for the next show when suddenly I got a phone call from Ken. He awkwardly said to me, 'Sorry, you're going to have to turn around.' The car had to change direction and drive me to Westfield Liverpool. The in-store was going ahead after all.

Throughout all the years I would go on to be a Sony artist, and despite becoming one of the highest selling artists on the label, I am not aware that Denis Handlin ever came to one of my shows. Perhaps that's why he didn't seem to have any understanding of what an actual performer has to go through. And if you have no voice and you're doing a show, it's the worst feeling. People are paying to come and see you, and if you can't sing properly they will sit there and be disappointed. Who could blame them if they never wanted to come to another show or buy another album? And if that happens it's deemed to be the artist's fault – it's the artist who has let down the record company by losing audience. Behind the scenes the label can say, 'She still has to do this and that.' My priority was to put on a great show for people who were prepared to spend time sitting in the audience, people who had spent money on a ticket. If I didn't have a voice I would be letting them down, and signing CDs in a store couldn't make up for that.

That was the start of a series of things that illustrated to me that my record company and I had different objectives.

After the finale of *The X Factor* I released the winner's single, 'Alive'. It was my debut single as an artist and, as happens regularly, Sony wanted to make a video clip.

They put me with a director to make the music video; he made the videos for many artists at Sony as he was essentially their full-time video director. And there's no other way to say this: he made a video that I thought was simply boring. It looked like no effort had been put into it. Everyone who had been following my X *Factor* journey was anticipating an impactful video to come out. This was my first music video after being crowned the winner. The fans had seen me in such amazing costumes and set designs so this was a big let-down. As soon as the fans saw it online they started posting comments, and those comments were bad.

Dannii Minogue stepped in at that point. She called Denis and said, 'We can't have that.'

I think Dannii felt a bit of responsibility for my career because we had come this far together; she was helping me and I guess was emotionally invested in developing my career. So then to suddenly have this label put out a video that could essentially ruin what we'd worked hard for, well, she wanted to do something about it.

So she said, 'Denis, we can't do that. We need a better video.' And I can imagine that would've been embarrassing for him.

Dannii rolled up her sleeves and said, 'I'll help put together a video treatment', which was a plan of how a new video could be made. She even said, 'I don't want any money for myself. Please put it towards the video.' She helped create this new video in a short span of time – she came up with a new creative concept and even flew over to direct it for me. And it was so much better this time round! I remain extremely grateful that Dannii cared enough to step in.

The next single was 'Super Love', although I often refer to it as my first single because that's the one I had a choice over; it wasn't associated with *The X Factor*. I loved that song and I was really excited to release it. It fitted me in so many ways and I loved that I was able to make creative decisions. I still feel so proud of that song.

I met with James Chappell, who was a music video director, and I told him the vision I had for the video, including the costumes. I wanted it to be colourful and fun, just like the song. We talked through the process and how we could make my ideas come to life. I worked with Heather again (she now works in the States with clients like Katy Perry). She was the costume designer I worked with for all those experimental costumes on *The X Factor* and she added her ideas on how to make this video as fun and eye-catching as I wanted it to be. I was new to the whole process of creating a music video but I had such a great time working on this because it was collaborative and I was able to experiment with what could be visually expressed. A lot was involved in this clip – we had several actors and extras, we made use of colourful smoke, crazy hair colours, a massive Slip 'N Slide, a drone and a grand piano on top of a hill overlooking Sydney, among many things. We created something from scratch that captured the energy of what I wanted. Most importantly, it was fun to put together.

'Gladiator' was the song after that. It was released in the days before Sony started to cancel my videos. And I mean cancel them *after* they were made.

To understand the impact of that kind of decision it helps to know that it wasn't just the record company who funded the music video – I did too. The way artists' agreements are constructed, there's something called a recoupable account. It's an amount of money set against the album or song, which accounts for the expenses that go into recording the song, mastering the tapes or making a video. In other words: the more that's done, the more money I had to earn back in royalties to pay for it.

Half of the cost of each music video went against my recoupable account, which meant that I had a right to see a video before the record company decided not to use it. But they never let me, and what I didn't know at the time was that if the record company decided not to use the video, I shouldn't have had to pay for it. Yet I did.

This started happening at the time of my second album, *Heart Beats*, which was my first Sony album of original songs. I wrote most of the songs on it, including 'Gladiator', and I was proud of what I'd achieved.

I wanted the follow-up single to 'Super Love' to be 'Gladiator', but Sony wanted it to be 'Living Dangerously'. I didn't want that to be my next single because I just wasn't connecting with it as much as I was connecting to 'Gladiator'. So I asked if I could go in and have a chat with someone at Sony, which seemed a logical thing to do to find a solution. The meeting was set but what I didn't realise at the time was that it was considered a big no-no to even ask for such a thing. When I asked my manager if I could have a meeting at Sony he said, 'Maybe,' and he set it up.

So I went in and said to Sony politely but firmly, 'I really would love "Gladiator" to be my next single,' and explained that I felt it was a stronger track to follow 'Super Love'. Sony seemed to agree, so I felt like that was a win, even if they weren't overly enthusiastic about the idea.

We went ahead and did a photoshoot for the single artwork. There was all this layering of metallic jewellery that looked like chains, and I had a pink wig on my head. Peter Brew-Bevan is an incredible photographer and it was exactly what I had envisioned for this song. My whole creative team were all so passionate about making this vision come to life. We worked hard and loved the collaborative process and ended up with an amazing result that I giddily imagined would blow everyone away, including my fans and my label.

After the shoot I had a gig to play in Singapore. While we were overseas my manager received a phone call from Sony saying that there was a problem. He told me that the single cover artwork hadn't been approved. The single was being released in a couple of days' time but it didn't matter: he said there would have to be a different photo. 'What do you mean? We don't have a different photo,' I said. 'That's the one we made for the single!'

Sony found an alternative option quickly. Their solution was to use the same photo that had been used for the cover artwork of 'Super Love' and change the colour from red to blue.

My fans – the Dami Army – notice all the details, so they started asking me why the same photo was being used for two different songs. I didn't have an answer for them. What was I supposed to say? That I had artwork that was interesting and perfect for the song that for some mysterious reason had to be thrown away?

Although there had been some hiccups already in my relationship with Sony, that was the first time that I felt devastated and confused. After all the work we'd done, and all the people who had been involved, it was heartbreaking. Everybody in my creative team had been excited about what we'd come up with, and here it was being trashed without a single reason or explanation.

I realise that there are things that happen in life that are much worse than a photo not being used, but as an artist I also know how many different parts go into making something a success and how many people rely on that success. The two years of the pandemic, when the music industry was basically on hold, revealed just how many people rely on music for a living. It's not just the artists. So a decision like the one Sony made affected not just me, but everyone involved. It wasn't about the money spent – and lost – so much as it was about the lack of regard for us all, and what it indicated about how things were going to be from then on. It didn't seem likely that Sony would start respecting my decisions if they weren't doing it already.

I now realise that the meeting where I had expressed my wish to choose a song that was different from Sony's pick would bring such consequences and that I would be paying for it for years to come. What felt like a cruel joke was only just beginning.

They wanted the next single to be 'Living Dangerously' – okay, I thought, this time they can have that as the single. I'd learned my lesson the painful way and paid the price of going against their decision. I didn't love the song as much as 'Gladiator' but it was still my song. How bad could it be? So I told the team that I agreed to the third single being 'Living Dangerously'.

I was hoping that this would appease Sony and that the nightmare would be over. Because the new album, *Heart Beats*, hadn't dropped yet, it would be the leading single for the album so the music video was important. This single and its video would drive this album.

So we made this crazy music video. We shot it in Adelaide. There were circus scenes, and a motorbike going around in a loop. There were rugby players and me dressed up in this rugby outfit. We were riffing on the 'living dangerously' theme. And there was a fun story going through the video.

Sony had seen the treatment and approved what we were going to do. There were multiple scenes in the video and they took lots of planning. They were long, gruelling days but it was worth it. I was really looking forward to seeing the video and eagerly awaited the first version to come through. Then apparently after a few days of the shoot, instead of the video edit, I was given the simple message telling me that Sony had watched the video and didn't like it. They said it couldn't be released. 'We need to protect your brand, Dami,' were their words. 'You need to make another one, we are protecting you.'

I hadn't seen the video and they wouldn't show it to me. They didn't want me to see it and to this day I haven't seen my own music video that I came up with and created. This also meant that I had a whole album about to be released and no video.

Sony put together a last-minute video shoot. I was about to travel overseas to perform so we had to shoot something overnight. We pulled together the styling, then went to a studio and did a very quick set-up with a piano and candles. And there was water on the floor. Even though it wasn't the video I'd wanted I desperately needed one to promote my album which I had been working on for months and months. It was another devastating and confusing time but I needed to make this album work so any video would be better than none, or so I thought.

But after I left the country I heard that Sony didn't like this one either. So I didn't get to release a video for that song, and that meant there was no video to coincide with the album release, because that was the single that was leading into the album. I never saw this video either.

My fans were asking me questions online: 'Where's the video? We saw the teasers. Why isn't it coming out?' Of course, I wasn't allowed to say anything. And up until now I have never said anything. But there were two videos made, at considerable expense – again, videos I was partly funding – and they were never shown to anyone outside of Sony. That's not only a waste of money but a waste of time, effort and creativity, and I think it's insulting to all the people involved that their work could be tossed aside like that. Amateurs weren't making these videos. They were professionals, just like me. The fact that management could just snap their fingers and say 'no' was enraging, and mystifying. I couldn't believe they had so much control over so many things, nor was it anything I could have dreamed of when I went on *The X Factor* and agreed to the terms.

That album, *Heart Beats*, still did well on the charts, but I felt like it didn't get the attention it deserved and it sort of fizzled out with no promotion surrounding it.

Barely a week after the album came out, my manager's line was, 'You know, things like this happen all the time. Let's move on.' For me it was incomprehensible to hear him say that. You can't give up on something you've created for months and months and months just because of one person who felt like crushing your dreams. Looking back, I wonder whether the lack of support was because of that one meeting that I had with Sony for voicing my difference of opinion. (How dare an artist have a say in choosing their single?!) Or I wonder if it was because it was an album of originals and Sony really wanted me to do something else – that is, they wanted me to take orders and record the songs they gave me, not songs I created myself.

While I couldn't know what was going on within my record company, I did know that I wasn't touring the album. Not because I didn't want to – *all* I wanted to do was play shows. The whole reason I went on *The X Factor* was to be able to get more gigs. But my manager, for some reason, wouldn't or couldn't organise a tour for me.

Fairly regularly I would ask, 'Will I be able to tour at any point?' and he would avoid answering the question. And for those who may wonder why I didn't organise the tour myself: my contract with Sony and my management didn't allow that. So I was stuck, not able to tour and not able to make my manager organise a tour.

The things I was asking for – touring, videos – weren't just to satisfy my artistic ego. I believed these things were important for my success as an artist, knowing that my success was also Sony's. My frustration was that at no point was the relationship in any way collaborative – my opinion wasn't sought or welcomed if I gave it, even though every single decision affected me. All I wanted was to be able to talk to Sony about the best way to do things or what the next steps would be. We were in a business relationship together so that would have made sense. Instead I was given orders and told to fall in line. I'm not a rebellious person by nature so it wasn't as if I instinctually wanted to go against what they said, I just couldn't understand why they wouldn't even consult me.

What my manager *was* able to organise was yet more corporate gigs. You may say that a gig's a gig, but at a 'Dami Im' show the audience is there to hear my music, while at a corporate gig I'm there to entertain an audience that's not necessarily interested in what I have to offer. I'm there to play music that the organisers want for their event, and they were usually the same predictable covers like 'Purple Rain' or 'Don't Leave Me This Way' that were crowd pleasers, and ones I had to sing over and over again.

So there I was with an album that I'd written and was proud of, the second album I'd released, and I had no shows to promote it or to perform for my fans. All I was doing was what my management and record company wanted me to do, which was play covers at corporate gigs – and then record the next album they wanted.

Sony decided that I needed to record covers of songs by the Carpenters. For those who aren't familiar with their work, Richard and Karen Carpenter were brother and sister, and they recorded iconic pop songs in the seventies and eighties, such as 'We've Only Just Begun' and 'Superstar'. They're well known to certain age groups but below a certain age there's not much awareness of them. By stating that they wanted me to record Carpenters songs, I think Sony had decided that I had one type of audience. But I knew that wasn't true – I received messages from all sorts of people, of all ages, from all over Australia. I didn't want to pigeonhole my audience and I didn't want Sony to either, but I didn't know how to change things. My manager was not fighting for what I wanted; no-one was. And eventually it was easier for me to give in on certain things because I could tell I had no chance of winning and I didn't want to exhaust myself trying. I cared about my fans, and as long as I kept that in mind I knew I could produce something great for them.

My *Classic Carpenters* album was really popular and ended up becoming Gold certified. But the process of making this album was again filled with frustrating hurdles along the way that made no sense. I worked with Bry Jones and Michael Tan who produced the album. We spent weeks in Michael's studio in Sydney's Potts Point recreating the songs. I didn't just want to replicate the original songs, I wanted to reinterpret them in a way that brought something new and different. If it was going to be pretty much the same as the original, wouldn't you just listen to the recording by the Carpenters? Of course, I didn't want to stray so far from the well-known originals to the point they became unrecognisable, but at the same time it was important that I brought freshness to them in some interesting way.

It took weeks of concentration and hard work from all of us to finish the selection of tracks for this album. Even though it wasn't ideal that I was in this position of making an album of covers, I poured my heart into the project and enjoyed the process of reinterpreting some of the beautifully written songs that were loved by millions of people around the world. When we finally felt it was finished, the tracks were sent over to Ross Fraser, who was my A&R, which stands for 'artists and repertoire'. An A&R representative's job is to sign new artists and help their artists in the process of recording and songwriting. It was also his job to take my album to Sony for final approval.

When I heard back from Ross a few days later it was bad news. Sony didn't like the tracks. We were told to re-record around 90 per cent of the album. I was confused and wanted to know what was wrong with them, and the answer was that 'they were not good enough'. What does that even mean? Over time I slowly began to realise that what he was actually saying was that he wanted them to be more or less a replica of the original Carpenters versions of the songs.

It's safe to say that re-recording the album the second time round was like swimming through mud. It was disheartening and so unfair and I didn't know how I could find the energy to do it. I felt terrible for Bry and Michael as well, who were feeling the same way as I did. We were so excited about the work that we'd produced together. None of us were expecting this outcome. But we saw no way out of the situation except to grit our teeth and finish the album the way Sony wanted.

CHAPTER TEN

Compassion

*T*hroughout my time on *The X Factor* I had the sense that I was there for a purpose other than simply competing in a television show. The way I came back into the show, after having been sent home, seemed to me to have a reason. Some may think I was reading too much into it but I was sure of it. I didn't just think, *I deserved it. I worked hard.* Because I felt a lot of people work hard towards big goals and dreams and they never have the opportunity I did on that show. I'd put in work over the years, true, but so had thousands of others. I couldn't help but believe it had all been part of God's plan – some may call it luck or coincidence – to find myself in that position. I realise that people can have a lot of talent, but that doesn't mean that they will find success on a TV show and find themselves suddenly famous and getting all this attention, and making money and being signed to a big label – it was almost a Cinderella story. So I thought there had to be a bigger purpose to why I had been given such success out of so many aspiring artists and I wanted to find out what that purpose was.

I almost felt bad, like I had taken someone else's opportunity. It was a type of imposter syndrome where one feels like they don't truly deserve their success. I was aware that I was having a positive effect on many people, especially those from communities in Australia who come from different cultural backgrounds. Prior to my time on *The X Factor* no-one with an Asian background like mine had been represented on a high-rating national TV show. Many of my friends with similar backgrounds who were cheering me on during the competition understandably shared with me their doubts, that even if I made it into the top three, the likelihood of me becoming a winner was slim. They felt they had never seen that happen on an Australian TV show before so it would be unlikely to happen to me. So it was amazing to surprise a lot of people and communities and prove that it's possible for a Korean-Australian to find success and popularity with a mainstream Australian audience. They all cheered me on and were celebrating my achievement as if it were their own. Whenever I had the opportunity to see my fans, like at an in-store signing,

I would see so many young girls and boys with different skin colours and ethnicities coming up to me with their eyes sparkling telling me that I was their inspiration. Parents thanked me for giving their kids confidence. I knew what that meant, and I loved it.

On the other hand, I began to realise that my success would create negative feelings for others. While most of my friends were celebrating with me, some people I used to know were starting to compare themselves to my achievements and I was told that a few people were even feeling like their lives were a failure. Gradually, my relationships with some people I'd known began to feel different as I was getting attention from everyone around me wherever I went, which left some feeling envious or even inadequate. I didn't want anybody to feel that way but these things were out of my control. My whole life had changed and there was nobody who could guide me in how to deal with this situation that I found myself in. I didn't *want* to attract attention when I was just living my life, at my church or at a birthday party or a friend's wedding, plus my lifestyle was crazy and hectic – I was flying to another city a few times each week for performances, photoshoots and other types of work, and wouldn't come home for weeks at a time. It became difficult to sustain my old life and relationships. Everyone was treating me so differently and there was nothing I could do to stop someone feeling envious or inadequate.

I questioned if my success was even a good thing. Was it making people feel happier or more miserable? I was confused and was desperate to find meaning; if I was given such a fate then I wanted to make sure I used it in a way God intended and do something positive with it, that it wasn't all just about me building a music career.

Eventually I reached the point where I could think that because I had worked hard I deserved to feel proud, to look back and think, *I did that*, and give myself a pat on the back – but being able to acknowledge my achievement was a few years away. And it took quite a process to get there because I always thought, *Anyone could have had this*. I didn't necessarily feel good about myself. I was constantly wondering, *Have I handled this right? What do I do next?* I didn't want to be the one who was wasting the winning lottery ticket that had been given to me for a kind of bigger purpose. But after a while, and the realisation that I could at least let myself be proud of what I achieved, it was nice to think, *I've done this and I'm actually stronger than I give myself credit for. So maybe I can handle it from here on as well.* That was a mind shift.

During the first few weeks after winning, I talked to my husband, Noah, about all of these things. He was the only person who watched what I was going through and understood how I was feeling. We agreed that this new profile could be an opportunity to do something good, and that maybe we could do something with an organisation called Compassion, which was special for both of us.

Compassion is an international Christian holistic child development organisation which has been running for over six decades and provides care to over two million children around the world. We had a long-time connection with Compassion as sponsors. I'd first heard about them and the work they do a few years before through my church. I decided that I wanted to sponsor children through Compassion when I was seventeen years old.

The first child I sponsored was a little girl in India called Somoli; I wanted to sponsor her because while the issue of child poverty was enormous, sponsorship meant I could help one child at a time even though I wasn't physically nearby and I was just an ordinary uni student living in Australia.

When Noah and I started dating I told him about Compassion and suggested that he sponsor a child. And even though he was a poor student, he started sponsoring a child in India as well. After a little while we wondered if we could go to India and meet our sponsored children, but at that point in time nothing came of it. After we married we decided to sponsor a third child in India, together.

After winning *The X Factor* I had the impetus to finally be able to organise a visit to our sponsored children, and I let my management know that I wanted to do this. They were happy to have their artists support charities they're passionate about, because they, and the artists, receive a lot of requests and it's much better for everyone if the artist already knows the areas they are interested in, regarding charity work.

Around that time I received a lot of phone calls from charities, churches and Korean communities, and people wanting me to make an appearance at their event. They found my phone number through connections and friends. I had to learn to say no without offending them – because often it wasn't the case that I didn't want to do whatever they asked for, it was simply that there were so many requests that I didn't have the time to do them all. It was tricky to manage well, though, because of course the people I said no to would see photos of me appearing at something and wonder why I wasn't able to attend their event or play at their church. And the short answer was: I would have needed to clone myself to do everything.

One request came in from my old pastor, who received a letter from an unknown person whose friend had cancer and didn't have many days to live. The pastor asked if I would go and visit this person, whom he said was a fan of my music. I wasn't trained in how to work with people who are dying so I was hesitant at first, plus I had received similar requests before. But for some reason I felt like this time I should go and meet this person and chat with him. Noah and I drove to the hospital where the patient was, which was about an hour away. He was a man in his sixties and he wasn't expecting to see us. He was surprised when we turned up by his bedside and was delighted to have us there, and we just sat and chatted about different things for a while. It was a meaningful thing to do and I was glad we were able to go and see him and give him a moment of joy in his final days, but obviously I couldn't do everything I was asked to do, even though I often felt guilty about that.

Compassion, however, was one organisation I was passionate about supporting. My manager set up a meeting with some people from Compassion and once we got in the room together I told them how long Noah and I had been donating to their organisation and how much we loved what they do.

'I'd love to support you any way I can,' I said.

They said, 'We actually tried to get in touch with you because we saw you were on the list of sponsors.'

They had emailed me while I was on *The X Factor*, once I was in the final rounds, asking if I'd like to be more involved with the organisation.

It felt like everything had aligned, and that this was meant to be God's plan. It was an exciting project to be involved with in the midst of all the confusion and all the transitions and questions I had about the changes taking place in my life at that time. Working with Compassion and helping these children was something solid, something I could believe in.

So I became a Compassion ambassador, which meant that I was committed to helping them on an official level, and that I would donate my time to do that.

As part of the ambassadorship I would play concerts in churches – and in the wake of *The X Factor*, due to the fact that no tour was organised for me, these were pretty much the only public performances I had. They weren't organised by Compassion, though, they were organised by little churches – which meant I was back to singing at my keyboard in a church, just as I had in Korea. I actually really enjoyed being in that church setting again – and the audience appreciated me a lot more than audiences had in the past!

After taking on the ambassadorship, Noah and I planned our first trip to India to go and meet our Compassion kids, in two different cities. Meeting them in real life felt surreal after sending letters to them and looking at pictures of them for many years. To actually speak with the children and their families and have meals with them, find out about the activities they liked and visiting their homes, was really special.

From that time we kept working with Compassion. Noah was even more passionate about this than I was. He'd say, 'Let's try to do a trip once each year.' And we did for quite a few years, visiting Uganda then the Philippines twice. Each trip was special and unique.

Uganda was planned before I knew I was doing Eurovision in 2016 and the trip happened right after Eurovision. I came second in Eurovision, which is the highest Australia has ever placed (and I'll tell you more about that later). That success was so much more than I had ever imagined and again I asked myself, *What does this mean? What do I do?* I felt as though the success was not – could not be – for me alone. I hadn't reached that point on my own, because there were so many people involved, and even for that reason it wasn't only my success. More than that, I felt it had to mean something.

But also, as with *The X Factor*, it freaked me out a little, because I felt the weight of responsibility. I'd achieved something huge, and a lot of people were watching. What could I do with that?

I thought, *This could be another opportunity to bring more attention to the work Compassion is doing with these kids.* So we pressed ahead with that Uganda trip, even though I knew my management and the label were both whispering, 'Why would she waste this opportunity and spend a week in Uganda?' But I knew it was the right thing to do.

We were able to take a whole TV crew from *Sunday Night*, and we were able to get a lot of publicity for Compassion and their work.

When I later went to the Philippines we partnered with Hope, which is a Sydney Christian-based radio station, and the aim of that trip was to get the whole village on the remote island of Masbate sponsored. Compassion was starting a brand new project in a village called Cabitan, where the average income was one US dollar a day, which was well below the poverty line. Compassion selected a local church in Cabitan to partner with to start this project, which meant that the Compassion support workers were 100 per cent locals from the village who already knew their community and their needs much more than any outsider or foreigner. The workers had already selected and signed up hundreds of children from the poorest families to be sponsored. Their parents had heard that the children were going to be able to attend school and receive medical support through the program, and be given meals and be visited and cared for by one of the support workers. This would benefit the whole village and empower the parents.

Just weeks before our visit to Masbate, Noah and I decided to sponsor a child from this brand new project in Cabitan. His name was Rodney, he was four years old and we couldn't wait to meet him. After taking two connecting flights into Manila, it took us another small plane to get to the island of Masbate, then another few hours driving. We drove through mountains overlooking the sparkling emerald ocean and through palm trees and rice fields. We had to be cautious not to drive over the rice grains that were being dried on the side of the road.

The long hours flew by as I was admiring the beautiful island that was showing off its paradise-like landscape. As we were getting nearer to our final destination we were stopped by a special sight we'd never seen before. A skinny boy around ten years of age was riding on the back of a grey water buffalo that was enormous. It almost looked regal, even though the boy was in his t-shirt and shorts with worn-out flip-flops dangling from his feet. We pulled over and got out of the car to say hello to the boy and soon he and his buffalo turned into a narrow, gravelly street. We decided to follow him in, walking behind the big creature, and that was when we learned that the boy was one of the older brothers of our sponsored child, Rodney!

We followed the boy and the buffalo all the way to where his house was. It was a tiny little hut made of dried banana leaves that could barely fit a couple of adults, let alone a family of five. Other children from the village followed us around with innocent curiosity, laughing and giggling.

A mother holding a sleepy child came out of the hut. She was tiny and looked frazzled. She woke Rodney up and the little boy seemed tired and uncomfortable in the humid, tropical heat of the day. Noah and I took out the gifts we had brought – toy cars, quilts and food essentials. We told her how excited we were to finally meet them and have Rodney be our sponsor child. The mother spoke back to us in Masbateño, but it was difficult to understand and we had to speak through an interpreter. We figured we shouldn't stay for too long as we realised that Rodney had been sick and needed to rest.

As we were leaving the house we couldn't help but notice a small mound on the ground close to their house.

'What is that?' I asked.

'It's a grave,' our interpreter told us.

We found out that a few years earlier the family had twins who had passed away as babies and the parents buried them near the house. As beautiful as the scenery and the picturesque mountains and the fields were, the paradise-like nature contrasted cruelly with the realities of poverty and the tragedy these people had faced.

The next day we went to visit another family from the village that had a child selected by one of the local Compassion workers, to be paired with a sponsor. After walking along about a kilometre of windy road through thick, tall grass, we got to a house made with rusty corrugated iron and thin wooden panels. There were six girls and two boys in this household, and they were being looked after by their grandma and aunt. Their mother had to move to Manila to find work and only came back to see the children once in a while.

The youngest of the children was John-Gerald, who was the candidate for Compassion sponsorship. He was four years old and although shy at first, had shown us his big personality by the end of our short visit. We were going to drive back to the Compassion project, and some of the kids wanted to come as well. We decided to give them a ride in our van.

As we started driving along, the children were laughing and giggling in excitement. We asked the worker why they were giggling.

'They have never felt air-conditioning before. This is the first time.'

Imagine living in the tropics, with over 30–40-degree heat with extreme humidity, like a steam sauna every day, then feeling air-con for the first time. Crisp air and the relief your body feels. It's something we take for granted, but such little things were bringing them so much delight.

When we got to the Cabitan church where they were running the Compassion project, some of the parents and their children had already arrived. As the village was establishing a Compassion project for the first time, it was a privilege to see the community bubbling with hope for a better future for their children. It wasn't just the practical help like food, education and medicine, although these are extremely important things that were desperately needed, but the idea that someone from the other side of the world would care enough for their child to help in a practical way. Donating money to them made them feel acknowledged and loved.

We attended the project a few times while we were there. I sang a couple of songs for them as well while playing a tiny keyboard connected to some old speakers, which reminded me again of my church-singing days when I had to make do with any kind of equipment. I watched the children and parents sing songs along with the director of the project, Pastor Ralph, playing guitar.

On the last day of our time there, while we were saying our goodbyes to everyone, we saw two boys run towards us. They were two of Rodney's older brothers. One of them had something in his arms.

When Noah and I walked towards them we were confused. They had brought a live chicken with them. It's not every day that you see boys running around with a chook in their arms. They were speaking to us but we couldn't quite understand what they were trying to say.

'Their mother wants you to have it,' the interpreter told us.

'What do you mean?' We were both so confused as we stared at the boys chasing the chicken that flapped its wings and started to run away.

'She is so grateful for all that you have done that she wants to thank you with this gift.'

We didn't know what to say. On the one hand it was bizarre that someone had offered us a live animal as a gift – of course the Australian quarantine rules would never allow this in a million years! On the other hand, we were so humbled by her generosity and heart to offer us something so valuable to their family. We had to explain to the boys that we couldn't take the chicken with us, but that we were so very grateful for their mother's generosity. I don't think I will ever forget that moment.

Our trip to Masbate was so memorable and special that Noah and I – and Ken Outch, who by this point had become my manager – decided that rather than going to another country, we would return to the same place and see the progress and continue to support the same village. This time I had another goal.

While I was at university I was really involved with my church, as I mentioned earlier. We used to do vision trips to the Solomon Islands once a year for a week at a time, visiting a sister church there. What I would see was these kids and youth and adults whose musical talent was incredible even though they weren't formally educated. They were provided with this opportunity to play music because the church had the equipment and it was a perfect way for them to be exposed to music, and they were naturally talented. I could see how much joy this music was bringing to the community and the youth there. A lot of the young people I met in the Solomons weren't able to go to school – although that did mean they had time to practise their instruments, and it was clear how powerful it was for them to have that access to music.

From that point on it became one of my burning dreams to help set up music schools for underprivileged communities. I wondered how we could get instruments to other communities where there might be so much talent but they might not have the access to resources to be able to nurture that talent. The thought of this made my heart leap, and I held on to it for many years, but since I'd become more focused on my music career I had forgotten about it. Once I'd seen the community singing together with Pastor Ralph leading on guitar, that dream came back to me. I felt my heart beat fast again at the thought of this – the beautiful community of people who were already so full of gratitude and joy even through their hardships. If the kids growing up there could have access to musical instruments, I knew they would just thrive.

On our second trip to Masbate, we took musical instruments with us. When we arrived at the Cabitan church, we saw hundreds of little children proudly wearing their Compassion uniforms. The community of new and familiar faces greeted us warmly. We gave the instruments to the project and the children were delighted. When I saw hundreds of kids holding their guitars and keyboards I realised that it was another full-circle moment. My heart was bursting with gratitude. Not everyone is able to see their dreams come true and I knew how lucky I was to have this opportunity, and to be able to share music with people who already have so much love for it.

We were able to continue our support back in Australia. We even did an online fundraiser to help

Pastor Ralph with getting additional equipment, and the Dami Army have been eager to contribute. When I think of the joy and hope that was radiating from the Cabitan community I can't help but think it was so worth it. All the confusion and the frustrations and isolation I went through following my *X Factor* win. I still believe that it was somehow all part of God's plan that I got to meet so many wonderful fans – the Dami Army – through the TV show, or Eurovision, or any of my music. These fans happily come on board with generosity every time I share something I believe is a worthy cause. For them I'm truly grateful.

CHAPTER ELEVEN

Eurovision

*T*he call from SBS, one of Australia's public broadcasters, came through on a Friday night. It was all very last minute and unexpected. When my manager rang to ask if I would like to accept the offer to represent Australia at Eurovision, my first thought was, *Oh. My. Gosh.* It was a big adrenaline rush – and obviously my answer was yes – a no-brainer! Eurovision is one of the biggest international platforms for singers and has produced musical legends like ABBA and Celine Dion. I found out later that SBS had initially chosen someone else for the global song contest, but that person fell through, so once again I was the second choice.

SBS would have had to tick multiple boxes before finally approaching me to be Australia's representative in 2016. I don't know what all the discussions would have been behind closed doors, but I do know what one of the reasons might have been. For over a year, my fans, the Dami Army, who had been growing in number and force, had been on social media messaging every person they knew who was related to Eurovision, saying I should be Australia's representative. I sincerely believe they had something to do with this opportunity coming my way.

I remember watching Eurovision for the first time at a sleepover with my friends when I was around fourteen and being all at once very confused and fascinated by the bizarrely eclectic performances and costumes. If you're not familiar with the Eurovision Song Contest, it is a global song competition that has happened annually since 1956 with participants from mainly European countries. It is broadcast live globally and is the longest-running annual international televised music competition and one of the world's longest-running television programs.

Australia had only been part of it for a year before I got the call. Guy Sebastian was our first competitor, and because of the special circumstances of his entrance, he was automatically put through to the finals. Initially, Australia's involvement was meant to be a one-off, commemorating the contest's sixtieth anniversary. After Guy came in fifth, it was announced that Australia would participate the following year as well.

For me to be the second Australian to ever compete at Eurovision was hard to believe. Having watched it over the years from a distance, suddenly I was going to be there. And by there, I mean in Stockholm, Sweden, on the famous Eurovision stage, competing against talented and creative artists from forty-one countries across Europe.

I knew I needed to find the right song before I could find the right costume and right staging. The duo behind my *X Factor* single 'Alive' – Anthony Egizii and David Musumeci of DNA Songs – had written a song and approached me about it. I went to their studio in Sydney to sing the song and to see if it would work. We spent the day in the studio recording the track and that was that. We knew straightaway it was a strong song and that it would be my Eurovision entry. 'Sound of Silence' was *the* song, but I wanted to make sure it was perfect.

After the song was chosen and before we left Australia to go to Sweden, I had another extremely busy period with back-to-back media and song promotion as well as actual preparations for Eurovision. I felt overwhelmed and tired from all the commitments but I kept feeling like the song wasn't as strong as it could be. While I was staying in Melbourne for media interviews and a L'Oréal photoshoot, I called Gary Pinto, the incredibly talented and most humble human being who was the behind-the-scenes vocal guru I met through *The X Factor*. We had stayed in touch since the show, and I wanted to workshop the song with him.

Noah had been watching other performers in the lead-up, especially those in Korea with impressive vocal range, and he believed that for a performance to stand out in a competition setting there needed to be moments of tension and intensity that would surprise people and give them goosebumps. I agreed with him. Even though 'Sound of Silence' is a great catchy song, it didn't have enough of those 'goosebump' moments. I had read some of the comments from Eurovision fans around the world and they echoed what Noah and I were feeling. When I called Gary he immediately came to where I was staying and helped me to find different phrases and variations to the original melody, to make the performance more interesting and dynamic.

Nailing the song was such a great feeling, but it was only the beginning. From there, we had to figure out the performance elements. I was working with Paul Clarke, who was responsible for making Australia part of Eurovision in the first place, and who was the Head of Delegation. He'd taken Jessica Mauboy over as a special guest performer, then Guy, and then he took me and produced my performance. The song was a ballad, which was great because it meant I didn't have to dance – I'm not much of a dancer – and I could focus on the vocals and connecting emotionally with the audience.

I made a mood board for my Eurovision outfit and put up photos of different outfit ideas. I wasn't exactly sure what I wanted but my ideas were based around sparkly things, hand-decorations ... I even had dresses with hoods on them. I shared these initial ideas with Heather, whom I'd been working with since *The X Factor*. I wanted it to be something different, interesting and stunning, and for it to have stage-worthiness. At the same time I didn't want it to be so stupidly outrageous that it detracted from the meaning of the song. Even though I do love and enjoy playing with 'stupidly outrageous' outfits, this time was different. That's where Steven Khalil, an Australian designer, came in. I went into his boutique in Paddington. Usually designers would need at least weeks, if not months, of notice in order to create a brand new gown but I was going to be leaving the country in a couple of weeks. He listened to Heather's and my thoughts and sketched a stunning gown on the spot. It was going to be a white gown made of Italian silk, but it would have thousands of Swarovski crystals sewn onto it which would reflect all the lighting on stage. A big split at the front to show my legs and bling jewels all over my right shoulder. We paired the dress with a seriously oversized hand piece going from my elbow to my hand from the couture jewellery brand House of Emmanuele. Overall, it was a mix of delicate femininity and Terminator-like power – if I punched with that hand it could make someone cry. Dramatic but elegant, exactly what I was picturing.

When it came to staging, Paul – who you could safely call the 'Eurovision expert' – came up with the idea of having me start my performance sitting atop a two-metre-high black box in the middle of the stage. We wanted it to look like I was hovering over a busy city. It was a very simple stage set-up – just me and the box – especially compared to some of the media favourites who had crazy graphics on stage. Russia even had a 3D climbing wall made of moving blocks. Our stage was quite the contrast, but Paul knew what worked and what didn't work on that stage, so we ran with it. When you're competing against forty-one other countries who are performing back-to-back in strict three-minute slots, you need to stand out. If you don't connect immediately you'll be forgotten, and I didn't want to be the performance that people used as a toilet break! Our idea wasn't to wow the crowd with fireworks, gimmicks or dance moves. We wanted to draw the audience in to focus and connect with me on an intimate level. This was our strategy and I loved it.

When we arrived in Sweden – after two flights, twenty-four hours and 15,088 kilometres – we hit the ground running. My team consisted of people from SBS and Blink TV, Noah, my parents, Paul, Liz my make-up artist, and Grant, a representative from Sony. My manager didn't come with me. Sony had told me they couldn't afford to cover the flights and accommodation for my make-up artist, so I asked if she could come instead of my manager, and they agreed. At that time, I knew my make-up artist would be more helpful for me than a manager, which I guess says a lot.

The Eurovision Song Contest is aired live across Europe, so each performer has a full week of rehearsals in the lead-up to the actual show. There's no room for error on live TV, so everything had to run like a well-oiled machine. From the very first rehearsal, you are watched by the Eurovision press pack, which is made up of journalists from all over the world. So going into a rehearsal isn't just about practising, it's about setting the tone for the whole competition. Paul had warned me about what to expect and explained how important it was to have some buzz around me. Eurovision acts are scored by a jury of music industry professionals from each country competing, and televoters at home as well.

Because of that, I knew I had to deliver something in the very first rehearsal that would make people talk. I had my variations to the song up my sleeve – thanks to my workshopping with Gary – and I tossed up whether

I should go full-force in my first rehearsal or save them for later. I decided to go for it. I wanted to cause a stir, and I did. The members of the press were surprised. They wrote articles and blogs about the Australian underdog being more than they had expected. It was a very good start.

What wasn't so good was the fit of my dress. In the first few rehearsals, my dress was so tight around my waist I could barely breathe and was on the verge of turning blue when I was sitting down, as I was meant to do for the first part of my song. It was so painful. And it only got worse when I was coming off the tall box to finish the song standing. The box also felt like sandpaper because it was covered in black glitter, and my gorgeous Italian silk dress would get caught every time I came off it.

We did four rehearsals in a row on that first day, and then went to a viewing room to watch them back. As I was sitting in the backstage room, I started to fade.

Paul asked, 'Are you okay?'

I said, 'I think my dress is too tight ...'

I couldn't breathe and I was turning blue!

I felt bad for Heather and Steven because we had to let the dress out so much. It was probably much bigger than was necessary, but my priority was my voice. I didn't care if my waist looked huge, I needed to be able to sing and to be comfortable. While the Eurovision wardrobe team made the alterations, we kept rehearsing and finessing my performance.

After every single run-through, we'd find something to fix or change. There were so many tiny details that had to be perfect, from the lighting to the timing of me coming off the box and the camera angles. There was a moment in my performance where I made these hand movements that looked like a hologram, and I had to get the timing exactly right without being able to see the visual effect on the stage. We rehearsed so much that week and with every rehearsal being watched by the press, I treated all of them like proper performances and it was exhausting!

As we were tweaking and tuning the version of the song I'd worked on with Gary, I received a call from Sony. 'Stick to the original,' they said. 'Don't change it.' I'd been experimenting with different notes and alternative melodies to get the most out of my performance, but Sony wanted me to sing the song exactly as it had been recorded, because that's how the song was released and they wanted it to sound the same. Paul was right there when I was on the phone call and after I had hung up, what he said to me was life-changing. 'I think you should do what you want to do,' he said. He didn't tell me to go against my label or to do as they said, he told me to go my own way, to trust myself and to own my performance. I didn't know I could do that. It was the first time I realised I didn't need to be at the mercy of Sony. It was also the first time I started to see that my label might have had a different agenda from mine. It honestly hadn't even crossed my mind before, which might sound naive. It became clear at that point that Sony were out to sell records in the short term, they weren't thinking of my career as an artist. It was a lightbulb moment.

Knowing that Sony wanted the song one way, and I wanted it another, made the stakes even higher. Coming into the semi-final, I knew I needed to be able to do the whole song with my eyes closed and my mind switched off, using muscle memory alone. I had to know that if my brain shut down with nerves, that my mouth would just keep singing. Luckily, that's exactly what happened. The night of the semi-finals was the most nerve-racking night of my life. A thousand times more nerve-racking than *The X Factor*. I could see that even the most seasoned artists felt the same going into the semi-finals. Someone who had been with Guy the previous year told me just how nervous he was when he competed the year before, which made me feel better.

I shook as I stepped onto the Eurovision semi-finals stage in Stockholm. The thought of having 200 million people watching me live – including all the Australians, who I was representing and who had woken up at 5 am to tune in to the show – was so much pressure. The reason the semi-finals are the most intense is because everyone wants to make it to the grand final. Once you're there, you've made it. The pressure lifts dramatically because even if you don't win, you've achieved something major. If I made it to the grand final, as Australia's second ever contestant and the first to have earned a place instead of being automatically put through, it would've been a good result. If I didn't, it would mean the whole team from Australia would have nothing to do for the next week. At that moment it felt like I was responsible for a whole group of people. I know it's just a music show, but I felt as though the fate of the country was sitting on my shoulders. That's a lot to carry for one little person.

I really wanted to do well. I remember looking out the plane window at the clouds on the flight to Stockholm and quite solemnly thinking to myself: *In a couple of weeks, I'll be coming home on this flight and I'll know what place I came in the competition. That number will stay with me for the rest of my life.* It was such a heavy thought, which sounds more like a soldier going into war rather than a performer on stage but that was how serious it was for me. I wasn't going to Eurovision to have a good time, I was going to deliver. I wasn't going to be okay if I got a mediocre result.

These were the thoughts running through my mind when I sang the first notes of 'Sound of Silence' on top of my box, in my Steven Khalil gown. I was frozen with fear, but I went into autopilot and trusted in the work I'd done in rehearsals. I surrendered to the stage. The Eurovision stage is massive. The stage and the stadium are unlike any TV studio I've ever been in – the scale is so large, and the cameras are everywhere, including flying around in the air like gymnasts capturing all the angles. It was as if I'd landed in another dimension with hundreds of lights pouring down like stars and cameras flying around as spacecrafts. Tens of thousands of people waving their flags, roaring and dancing, all of them high on music. It felt like a dream, even as I was standing right there.

In a space so grand, the audience could feel far away, but they didn't. As soon as I sat on my box, there was a cheer. It was the biggest rush of raw energy and encouragement that I'd ever experienced. As a performer, there's nothing better than the support of a crowd – and the crowd at Eurovision was the most enthusiastic and fun audience I've ever experienced. In the semi-final, the performers could feel how much they were or weren't getting from the crowd. I had to be lifted and pre-set carefully by my crew during the commercial break. As soon as my box was wheeled out, I knew that I was liked and supported. The energy from the cheering and chanting crowd reached me like electricity in my body, and that took my performance to the next level.

I left it all on the stage. I gave the semi-final performance everything I had and then some. It felt so good just going for it from the very start of the song and getting the crowd excited. I decided to sing the song my way and it paid off. It was the scariest but the most thrilling experience. There is nothing else like it. I made it through to the grand final and, not only that, I found out that I received the top score!

One of the questions about my performance that I get asked frequently is how I got off that box. One moment I was sitting on top and the next moment I'm standing on my feet. It's like a magician's trick where once you know how it's done, you realise it was really nothing. A part of me wishes I'd kept it a secret. But it really was a simple trick where I got carried off by two muscly men while the cameras were shooting from far above. It was a precisely coordinated routine that was only possible because of all the rehearsals.

There were four days between the semi-finals and the grand final. Those days were for more rehearsing, but it was also for schmoozing. There were the press interviews, the club performances and the parties. The Eurovision Club was in the Eurovision Village, and it went off every night. I imagine the energy would be similar to the Olympic Games – if not a little more theatrical. It was Disneyland for performers and music fans.

Acts were expected to practise their routine during the day, and party at night. There were a lot of different Eurovision parties, hosted at various embassies. For example, the Australian Embassy would host a party for us and invite guests from the other countries and make the most of the celebratory atmosphere. Artists would go to other people's parties and events to win votes, as you can't vote for yourself so your success depends on your alliance with the expert judges from different countries. I knew it was important to be involved and to get to know the other countries, but I was conscious of managing my energy levels. I was also the only act battling jetlag because I'd travelled from Australia, whereas everyone else lived around the corner in Europe. For an introvert like me, it was all pretty overwhelming, but I tried to focus on my performance above all else.

Stockholm is such a beautiful city and I wish I had been able to enjoy it more, but I was at work, not on a holiday. My parents were with me, as well as Noah, so we had a couple of nice meals together, but it wasn't like I could just relax and enjoy my time there. I spent most of my time away from the studio in my hotel room. I knew sleep was the most important thing for my voice, so I forced myself to be boring (which wasn't that hard) and slept as much as I could. I drank warm tea with ginger, lemon and honey and had my humidifier running around the clock. I was conscious of how much talking I was doing – especially in loud environments where I had to strain to be heard – and tried to speak as little as I could to protect my voice.

I tried not to look at too many online commentaries. It was part of keeping laser-focused on my physical and mental stamina like an athlete, so I avoided googling myself or looking at the betting odds, and yet I couldn't help but find out that I was one of the Top Five favourites. It was so exciting – and I was quite impressed and amazed – but I also felt the pressure at the same time. That old chestnut!

Performing in the Eurovision grand final was the most exhilarating experience of my life. I loved it. The energy from the crowd was glorious; euphoric, even. Unlike the extreme tension I felt in the semi-finals, I could relax and soak it all up. Backstage in the green room, the teams from each country in the grand final sat in a circle with the cameras pointed on them to catch their reactions to the other performances. When Justin Timberlake came out to perform, we all let our hair down and danced together in a big conga line. Everyone in my team was partying and dancing, living out their camp fantasy, dancing to Justin Timberlake at Eurovision. It was a lot of fun ... until they started announcing the results. That's when things got real.

I remember the producers told me to keep my in-ear pack on, which is the device we use for the performance to listen to ourselves. I thought it was a little strange because I'd finished my performance, but I figured we must have all been keeping them on. Later, I realised it was only me and one other performer who still had them on. As the results started to come in, we kept getting the highest points – twelve – from each country. The twelves were rolling in, and the cameras were squarely pointed on us. We didn't realise we were going to get the most top points, so everyone was just so excited. I was sitting next to my dad, and I had to keep asking him what was happening. I have pretty bad eyesight, so I couldn't actually see the scorecards. Dad was crunching the numbers for me – ever the analytical member of the family – and at one point he told me we were on top. On my other side was Grant, the Sony representative, who had been partying harder than anyone just moments before, but who was suddenly very still. I could see him getting paler and paler as the results came in. I could almost read his mind. *Holy crap*, I imagined him thinking. *What are we going to do? We're not ready for this. We haven't prepared to win.* He was freaking out and that was equally funny and terrifying.

After all the jury votes had been counted, we were at the top. I was frozen with shock. But the public votes still had to be counted, so we had a moment to consider what it would mean if we won. It would be a first in the iconic contest's sixty-one-year history. There were rules in place that if Australia were to win, the contest would not be held in the Southern Hemisphere the following year (as it was tradition for the winning country to host the next competition), and that instead we would co-host with a country within the European Broadcasting Union. It was a lot to process in a short amount of time.

It all happened very quickly. We were at the top, and then we weren't. After the public votes came in, we slipped from first place to second, just behind Ukraine, who were being represented by an artist named Jamala, who performed a song called '1944'. One minute I was winning, the next I wasn't. It was shock, followed by even more shock, but of a different kind. My euphoria from performing had turned into a dizzying disbelief that I might actually win, and then to the disappointing reality that I wasn't going to. It's a cliché, but it really was a roller-coaster of emotions.

In my interviews after the results were announced, I could barely speak. There were no words, just tears. Mostly happy tears! I was feeling so many emotions, but the main one was still shock. 'What just happened?' I kept asking myself. I was so happy to have placed second, but because there was a moment where I thought I was going to win, it wasn't so simple. I hadn't lost, but I hadn't won either, so it was hard. I was conscious of looking disappointed and sounding like a loser, when only a small part of me felt that way – and only because we'd been so close to winning. I tried to manage my emotions, but there were so many of them.

It felt like an explosion had gone off inside me with bursts of relief, joy, excitement and exhaustion. The pressure of the past two weeks, and months of preparation, was over. It was all over. Just like that. So, when the journalists started asking me questions about placing second and if I was still going to push ahead with my upcoming gig at Rooty Hill RSL, I just cried. I hadn't had time to process the past ten minutes, let alone think about the future, so I found it difficult to express what I was feeling and thinking. I was a bit of a mess.

My eyes were wide but empty. Since then, I've seen the same blank expression on the faces of Olympians and tennis champions in their post-competition interviews.

After such an intense experience, it's pretty understandable that someone wouldn't be in their right mind. It almost felt like an out-of-body experience. I'd been running on adrenaline for so long, all I wanted was to crawl into a corner and sit by myself.

That night, I went out with the Australian crew for celebratory drinks. I ordered my lemonade and hugged and cheered with everybody. There was such camaraderie in that moment. I still hadn't processed what had happened, it was all a blur, but what I knew was that we had achieved something incredible – coming second place at Eurovision. It was a result that was more than what anyone could have imagined and I felt so proud and relieved that I had given my all for the whole team. Paul came up to me at that moment and asked me, 'Do you want to do this again?' I wasn't so sure what he meant or if he was being serious. Obviously, he was already thinking about the next year.

After the bars closed everybody went to the Eurovision Club and partied but I was utterly depleted. 'I'm sorry, I've got to go and rest,' I told my team. I don't like to miss out, but I physically couldn't stay up and not sleep. I don't know how people do that. So, I celebrated my Eurovision second place with my pillow in my hotel room.

* * *

The morning after Eurovision, I slept in. When I eventually got up, I went out to brunch with the Australian team who'd been working on Eurovision with me, including Paul, the SBS team and my Sony representative. On our way to the cafe we walked past a newsagency, and I saw my picture on the front cover of the Swedish newspapers. It was crazy! If I had thought it was all a dream, I didn't anymore. It was real. I had come second in the world's biggest song contest.

Sony was happy with my result; most importantly, Denis was happy. They didn't say anything about how I defied them and sang the song my own way instead of exactly the way it was recorded. The single charted not only in Australia but globally, and my upcoming tour sold out.

At the cafe, which was Australian-owned, all the tables were celebrating with me. We did a 'cheers' with orange juice, and even the Swedish customers recognised me. It was such a great celebratory energy. From back home in Australia I was getting messages – it felt like from every single person in the country – congratulating me. Even the prime minister, Malcolm Turnbull, and opposition leader, Bill Shorten, sent me tweets saying well done. It felt like all of Australia was really behind me and excited for me.

One by one, the Australian team started to leave for their flights home, and I wished I could have joined them to get back to all the excitement. But I happened to be staying on in Stockholm for an extra week because I'd booked a co-writing session with some Swedish writers. Obviously, we'd made that plan not factoring in that I might have done really well. We clearly hadn't backed my chances. In hindsight, we should have maximised the time straight after Eurovision in Australia and ridden the success. It was the peak of my career, and I was stuck in a studio in Stockholm. I rang my manager, back in Australia, and told him I felt like I should be capitalising on the opportunity, instead of writing behind closed doors.

'This is the biggest moment of my career. I'm getting so much attention for what just happened, I feel like we should make the most of that and that I should be doing more press in Europe, or coming back to Australia,' I said.

'I thought you didn't like press because it was tiring?' he replied.

'No. I might have said that when I didn't have any time to sleep or prepare for Eurovision and I was worn out by all the interviews, but this is different,' I explained.

'What do you want? Do you want to come home?'

'I don't know. What's the best strategy here? I just know I want to maximise this time,' I said, deferring to his expertise.

'Let's just sit tight and see what happens,' he said.

Spoiler alert: nothing happened. I stayed in Stockholm and spent the week in the studio writing – even though I wasn't in the right headspace to be doing that. I'd had so much adrenaline pumping through me after the competition and it all went to waste. It was a really weird feeling. I hit a wall, my mood was low and my body wasn't coping.

When I had arrived in Stockholm two weeks earlier, the entire city was decorated with Eurovision flags, posters and billboards. In the week after the competition, I saw people pulling down all the decorations. It was all over, everyone was gone, but I was still there. It felt quite sad.

I rang Paul, who had left Sweden to go to London. He asked me how I was doing, and I wish I could have told him I was on top of the world. That's how I should have been feeling after such a phenomenal experience and wild success. Instead, I told him I felt lost.

'I'm sad it's all over, and I don't really know what I'm going to do now,' I admitted, adding that I was disappointed with how my management was handling things.

'It seems like your management isn't really looking after you, to be honest,' Paul said.

'Yeah, but what can I do? I can't just leave,' I said.

'Why not?' Paul replied.

'He'll be upset,' I said.

'He will be fine. You can do whatever you want.'

It was another lightbulb moment – just like when Paul told me I should sing 'Sound of Silence' the way I wanted to. It honestly hadn't crossed my mind that I could ever leave my management. This might sound dramatic, but I felt like I was in a relationship where I couldn't break up with my partner because it would hurt him too much. I didn't want to upset anyone. Besides, I didn't know a music career without Sony. I had been locked into my contract with them since the day I won *The X Factor*, and they had a five-album option. I'd released three albums with them, so there were still two options left.

I hadn't been inside the music industry before *The X Factor*, so I didn't know how things worked behind the scenes and that there were other ways of doing things. After my phone call with Paul, I started to think about the possibility of getting a new manager and what that would look like.

I have a lot to thank Paul for. Working with him on Eurovision was such a special time, and I credit him for our success, because he was so smart, prepared and supportive. He helped me through every single stage of the competition. It was the first time in my career that I felt like I was being looked after and respected as an artist. It was a big deal for me – and a wake-up call of sorts that I needed to consider my options going forward.

In that sense, Eurovision was life-changing for me in more ways than one.

CHAPTER TWELVE

Dreamer

*M*y Eurovision dress is now on display at the Australian Music Vault in Melbourne, alongside Chrissy Amphlett's iconic schoolgirl tunic, and lyric sheets written by Nick Cave. That dress tells an extraordinary story of a girl exceeding expectations on the world stage. You can see how big the waist looks because I needed the space to use my full vocal range, and you can also see the pulls in the silk from the sandpaper-like box prop. Under the seams and stitches, the dress also tells the story of a girl coming into her own and learning to stand up for herself.

When I got back to Australia after Eurovision, I was very confused. A seed had been planted in my mind about getting new management, and I started to question everything – both figuratively and literally. One day, I called my manager and asked him outright what his role was.

'What do you do? Why do I have you as manager? What role do you play here?' I questioned him. I was totally genuine. I wasn't being flippant or passive-aggressive, I wanted to know what he did. My manager's response was punctuated by *ums* and *ahs*, and it didn't really answer my question.

Over the years, I'd become used to my manager's empty promises. I came to take everything he said with a grain of salt. In our very first meeting after I won *The X Factor* and was signed to Sony, he gushed about all the gigs he had booked for me, how much travel I had ahead of me, and how I was going to need a bigger suitcase. In that moment, he sent someone from his office out to Myer to buy me the biggest suitcase they had in the store.

'How do I pay for this?' I asked with a laugh, totally unaware of how things worked.

'No, it's my present for you,' he explained. I now know it probably would have come out of the Sony account.

Another time, I told my manager that Noah had burned one of his shirts while ironing it. 'Oh, I've got an amazing laundry lady who can fix that for you!' he said, taking the shirt from Noah. We never saw the shirt again. There were so many things that were said but never carried out. So many grand plans that were never executed, and so many promises that never came to fruition.

Upon my arrival home – after a long week stuck in Stockholm – I was excited to connect with everyone who had supported me at Eurovision and to do something special with my fans. Paul had suggested doing a homecoming performance at the Opera House, but Sony apparently didn't have any plans for me. The very first appearance I had after taking out second place at the most-watched song contest in the world was a corporate gig in a conference venue in Canberra. What an anticlimax! I vividly remember singing 'Sound of Silence' to a room of men in suits, cutting steak and making small talk. It was pretty depressing – and felt like a stark contrast to the joy I had felt at Eurovision.

The worst part of my 'welcome home' gig was that I was on my own. Nobody from my management team travelled with me to Canberra, so I didn't have any support. I could have used it. There was an awkward moment before the performance where I was getting changed in a room backstage and had a wardrobe malfunction. The venue security guard was in the room watching me as I was half undressed and I had to ask him to leave. That wouldn't have happened if I'd had someone from my management team on the ground with me.

After that, I managed to get my next few corporate bookings cancelled. It didn't make sense to me that I was meant to be doing random company lunches that had been booked months ago, when there was so much interest in me. In music, there are plenty of times when people don't care as much, that's the nature of the business. So when there is interest, you should make the most of it. No-one, not Sony nor my manager, seemed to be looking out for my career and it forced me to have some difficult conversations. It was a really stressful time, especially for an introvert like me who hates conflict of any sort. I steeled myself. I told my manager I wasn't happy with how he was handling my career.

My manager said he was going to schedule a meeting, that he would assign a senior manager in the company to work with me exclusively and that he would speak to Denis, the boss at Sony.

I remember back in 2015 when my manager organised for me to play two shows in Korea and China at the Australian embassies over there. It was a big schedule with multiple flights to places I'd never been to before. On trips like that, someone from the management company would normally accompany me. The day before my flight, I asked my manager who was coming on the trip with me.

'Oh, I am. I'm coming tomorrow. I'll be there,' he said, flustered. 'I'll meet you there.'

Clearly, he wasn't coming. It takes a whole day to fly to Korea, so he could hardly 'meet me there'. When I arrived, I asked my manager when he was getting in, and he assured me he'd be there the next day.

'Sorry, I got held up,' he said the next day. It was at this point I realised he definitely wasn't coming and that I was going to have to do the shows and work with people I'd never met or spoken to all on my own. Luckily Noah was travelling with me, so that was something, but I still felt let down. If my manager had said from the beginning that he wasn't going to be able to make it, I could have been put in touch with the team on the ground and communicated with them directly, so it wasn't such a stressful experience for me.

When we arrived in China, someone from the Australian Embassy picked us up and asked where my manager was. I had to tell them he wasn't coming. The embassy worker had expected him to be there, just like I did. They thought it was quite unprofessional of my manager not to turn up, and to send an artist on their own.

The moment I realised my manager wasn't coming to meet me in Korea like he'd said, I sent him an email. 'Hey, I'm actually a bit disappointed that you would do this to me, that you would promise me something and then not do it,' I wrote. 'You could have at least told me, instead of leaving me hanging like this in a random environment.'

We then had a phone call where he was angry at *me*. I couldn't believe it – this was the first time I'd experienced behaviour like this from my manager. I was so upset and it felt like this was the moment the relationship started to fall apart.

Reflecting on the situation, I think the biggest issue with the way my career was being handled was the management structure. My management company – Parade Management – was owned by Sony. A manager is meant to work for the artist – not the record company – but that wasn't the case at Parade. It was a clear conflict of interest. My manager couldn't have my back if he had to have Sony's. And so, if me doing corporate gigs made Sony more money because they got a bigger cut of those shows than others, that was his priority.

It took me a long time to realise that my manager had less power over me than I thought. As an up-and-coming artist, it felt like my manager and the bosses at Sony had the power to end my career. They also had the power to make my career, but they weren't very proactive with that. I didn't want to take the chance to see if they'd be proactive in destroying my career if I called them out, but I knew something had to be done.

My saving grace during this tense time was my trip to Uganda with Compassion. That visit had been planned before I knew about Eurovision and even with the triumph of my second-place win – and my confusion over my management – I wasn't going to back out of this trip. I was going to Uganda and fulfilling my commitment with Compassion, no matter what. After all, what was the point of my success if it didn't mean something, if it didn't help someone other than me, or if it didn't make a difference. The trip to Uganda really put things in perspective. As stressful as it was knowing what was waiting for me at home, I was happy to escape my reality and focus on something bigger than me. My soul was grateful.

When I did return to face reality, I was given the gift of an unexpected ally. My prayers were answered in the form of Ken Outch. I knew Ken from Sony where he was a marketing manager, and from when he worked on promoting my first album back in the day. He was someone I trusted and who had integrity. Ken had shown an interest in management, so Sony's plan – after I'd voiced my concerns – was to move him over to Parade and sort things out.

I met Ken at the cafe of the Sydney hotel I was staying in. When he asked me what was happening, I burst into tears. I didn't mean to – and I tried very hard not to – but all the emotions I had bottled up came pouring out. I can't remember exactly what I said in response to Ken's question, but I explained that I didn't think my management had been very helpful to me or my career. Ken hadn't realised how bad things had been for me and he immediately stepped in to help. He took over managing me and things felt better straightaway. I wanted to make things work. Not just because I still had two album options with Sony – but because I felt like Ken was fully behind me.

My very first album tour started in the July of 2016, just as Ken took over my management. My 'Yesterday Once More' Classic Carpenters tour started in Victoria and included thirty-four dates across Victoria, New South Wales, Queensland, South Australia, Tasmania, the Australian Capital Territory and Western Australia. My Carpenters album may have been my third album with Sony, but as I've explained, it was my first tour with them. Considering the reason I auditioned for *The X Factor* in the first place was because I wanted to perform more, not being able to tour my first two albums was especially cruel.

Hitting the road and performing was an amazing feeling. So, too, was having a manager who I felt like I could really communicate with. I knew Ken would always tell me the truth – even if it was bad news from the powers above. It was so refreshing to have genuine discussions and planning of my career for the first time.

Preparing for my very own tour was beyond exciting. It had been three years since being signed to a major record label and finally I got to perform, not at a corporate event or a function, but for my fans who had loved and supported my music for years. I had a lot of learning to do. Which songs should I play? Do I want three musicians or seven? Which sound engineer and lighting technician? What equipment do I take? Which venues should I play? How many dates? I definitely didn't know all the answers and just like anything else, it took a lot of trial and error to work out what was best.

I remember the very first show was at Frankston Arts Centre and I was so nervous. I opened up to the audience during the first couple of songs, that this was my very first show of the tour and that if it sucked then I'd fix it for the next show. The audience laughed and applauded with warmth. They were engaged through the whole of the two-hour show, cheering, laughing and crying. Not only did I love playing and singing my music, but I loved making jokes, telling stories and just connecting with them. This is what I dreamed of when I decided to quit classical piano and pursue singing. It felt like I had reached a milestone.

After every show on the tour, I would do a signing and meet my fans. Often the queue to the signing table would stretch on for metres. It's always nice to meet people who enjoy and support your music, and to feel their excitement in person. As an artist, you never really know how people will receive your music. It's always humbling to hear stories from people who say that one of my songs helped them through a difficult time, or reminds them of their late mother, or makes them dance/smile/cry. I have had fans burst into tears when they meet me – it's usually the younger ones, the teenagers, who freak out. It's very cute. In the regional towns on the tour, I found it so interesting to see how many different people came to my shows. There really isn't one 'typical' Dami Im fan, they come from all walks of life, and I love that.

As much as I enjoy meeting fans after gigs, I have to admit it can be quite tiring. Often, I just want to chill out or celebrate with the band after a show, but I know how meaningful those moments are to the people who've come out to see me sing and lined up to say hello. On the last night of the Carpenters tour, in Perth, the show finished at 10 pm, which was midnight on the east coast. I was already out of my body with exhaustion because of the time difference, so by the time I got through the signing line two hours later, I was beyond tired. I could tell how much everyone appreciated it though – they all thanked me for coming – so I slept well knowing that I'd made my fans happy.

The tour was a brilliant experience – I really enjoyed it and felt like I was making progress. My career was heading in the right direction, and I felt in control of it.

By the end of 2016, I was more confident than ever. I released an original single called 'Fighting for Love', and did a fashion shoot with *Stellar* magazine to mark the start of a new era in my career. I told the journalist on the set of the photoshoot, 'For me, "Fighting for Love" is about empowerment. I've always wanted to sing about love and spread hope.' I was wearing a cut-out Christopher Esber dress and platform Fendi shoes. 'It's kind of scary when you are bringing original songs out into the world. I have to embrace that vulnerability and see what happens.' I added, 'I feel more confident now because people treat me with more respect. There are days when I'm like, "I can do this. I've got this!"'

Despite all the success I'd had with 'Sound of Silence' and my original work, Sony insisted that I had to make another covers album after *Classic Carpenters*. It was frustrating. I shared my frustrations with Ken, and he fought the good fight for me, but Sony were adamant: it had to be a covers record. Ken told me if we did one more album of covers, we could negotiate to do originals the next time around. It was a compromise, but it was far from ideal.

In fact, it was a real struggle. I felt like once again I was wasting the halo of opportunity that Eurovision had given me. I knew the fans I'd made from Eurovision would want original songs from me, but what could I do? I decided to do a pop jazz album – because at least I enjoyed singing that type of music – and settled on the album name, *I Hear a Song*.

I managed to record two original songs to go on the album, including the above-mentioned title track, 'I Hear a Song'. If only my fans knew how much I had to fight to release that track – and to get through making the album at all.

At first, the A&R representative at Sony had put a producer on the album who I didn't feel respected me at all. I felt like they thought they knew better than me. It seemed as though they were dismissing me because I was a pianist and a singer. I wanted to play the piano and sing the songs to interpret the music in that way, but they would tell me it wasn't working because I was playing on the tracks. They said they needed to find a better piano player.

Realising that I wasn't understood or even respected by this producer, I knew I couldn't work with him on the project. But the producer and the A&R manager decided that I should sing with a band that they had put together, and I would not be playing the piano. That's the way the producer had worked in the past and he wanted to do the same thing again. I really didn't want to do it that way. I knew it was a waste of time, but I only had one choice – to try it his way.

Making an album should be a collaborative process with mutual respect. It didn't start out like that on *I Hear a Song*. A lot of time and money was wasted before the A&R manager was fired and I was assigned a different producer. Eventually – after that incredibly frustrating process – I got to work with Rick Price on the album. From the second I met Rick, it felt better. He respected me and he listened to what I wanted. It's not rocket science. I'm not a difficult or demanding artist to work with, I'm open to working with people, if those people are open to working with me. Music is a collaboration, not a dictatorship. Working with Rick was like a breath of fresh air.

Rick is a songwriter and a musician as well as a producer, so he just gets it. He's based in Nashville, so I travelled to his studio there and got to experience America in the fall. The leaves on the trees were turning golden and there were squirrels in the backyard. It was around Thanksgiving and the atmosphere was so beautiful. I loved being in Nashville and experiencing all the music – and the honky-tonk bars.

In Rick's studio, we worked on all the arrangements together as a team, and I got to play with some incredible musicians from Nashville. The bassist we worked with had toured with the legendary jazz pianist Diana Krall, and he brought this special groove, drama and swag to the album. It all came together super quickly. And, oh yeah, I played piano on every single track. It felt like redemption. I knew I was good enough to play piano on my own album – I had a degree in it, for heaven's sake – but being told by the first producer that we needed a 'better' player was insulting. In the end, the songs spoke for themselves – backed up by my piano-playing.

In the lead-up to the release of *I Hear a Song* in 2018, I felt like I needed to issue a warning to listeners. 'Before you listen to the album it might look like an unusual combination of songs, but I recorded every tune with the same desire, which was to share the stories of these amazing women, the most raw and simple way, through a microphone and my fingers on the black and white keys,' I said.

The album went to number one on the Australian Albums chart and was well reviewed in the Australian music media. Acclaimed journalist Cameron Adams wrote, 'While *The Carpenters* [cover album] made her sound old before her time, this one works well. Jazzy gems from everyone from Beyoncé to Nina Simone to Norah Jones to Bonnie Raitt. Two originals suggest Dami is more down with "bebop" than "dance pop" now.'

To be honest, I wasn't even sure what my own sound was. The music I was interested in writing wasn't accepted by my label. It was hard. It made me question whether I could write something that people wanted to listen to. When it came to music, I knew what I liked and what I didn't like, but I couldn't do what I truly liked. It made me second guess every chord progression and every lyric I wrote. All that doubt really took the passion from me.

Before *The X Factor*, I had written songs on my own, but I'd never co-written with anyone before. After I got signed, I was thrown into a room with a group of strangers and the task of writing a hit pop song. There was so much pressure for me to write something that was radio-friendly, something that Sony liked, and something that sounded like me. What is 'me'? It's taken me years to answer that question – and the answer is ever-evolving. But back then I didn't know, and on reflection, co-writing probably wasn't the best way for me to find out.

At every single co-writing session, I would end up crying in the bathroom. No-one knew this and I kept it that way because it was embarrassing, but I couldn't help it. I'd freak out and panic, and the more I tried to keep it together, the more I would freak out and panic. I wasn't in the right mindset to make the most of the co-writing sessions. On a personal level, sitting in a room with strangers was stressful for me. I needed to have more confidence than I did at the time. On a professional level, I couldn't wrap my head around how I was supposed to make something with people I didn't know in a situation I hadn't been in and using a process I hadn't experienced. Some people can be thrown into a writing session and be fine. I wasn't. I put so much pressure on myself and had too many thoughts going through my mind.

I have perfect pitch and I'm a professionally trained musician, but I still felt like I couldn't contribute. Meanwhile people who didn't know much about music at all were coming up with songs. It messed with my head.

I dreaded my writing sessions in the same way university students hate group assignments. I felt like I spent the sessions desperately trying not to panic instead of actually connecting with something deeper, which is what I used to do when I wrote music on my own. I lost my connection and stopped being able to tap into my creativity. After a while, it felt like I lost the ability to write at all. The songs that came out of those sessions weren't true to how I wanted to sound. I was going with the flow and doing whatever sounded catchy. I was going through the motions, but I wasn't enjoying the journey and I wasn't particularly happy with what came out of it. For so long I had wanted to write and create my own music, but I started to doubt if that was even possible. *Maybe Sony are right. Maybe I should just stick to covers. Maybe that's all I can do,* I thought.

It was only after Eurovision that I decided to go back to my roots and to write on my own again. For the first time in a very long time, I remembered what it was all about and what I actually wanted to say. That's when I wrote 'Dreamer'. It's quite an incomplete, rambling sort of a song, but I wrote it on my own. It's mine. Sony released 'Dreamer' at the end of 2018, and I performed it live at the *Eurovision: Australia Decides* show on SBS at the start of 2019. The track is about my frustrations with my label, but I'm not sure if they realised that at the time. In the lyrics, I found my voice again ...

I'm not a puppet who moves with your hand
I'm not that woman who begs for command
I'll never settle for what's second best
I know what I want, I know who I am

I'm one of those people with too many questions
Is there meaning in my endless pursuit or is it just
an addiction
I'm searching for ways to describe the rivers of
thoughts in my mind
Not even a book full of words could say what's
inside

I'm not that stupid, don't need your advice
And I have a vision and I know the price
If I had to battle I'd fight to the end
I know what I want, I know who I am

CHAPTER THIRTEEN

The Boardroom

*I*n my post-Eurovision world, 'Dreamer' was the start of a stronger and more confident Dami. Following my success on the world stage and all of the realisations that came with that, I felt like I developed better mental strategies, I grew up a lot and stopped caring quite so much. I became better at coping with my own anxieties and emotions. It took a long time, but I found myself. As the song goes, 'I'm a dreamer, a believer'. And slowly but surely, I started to believe in myself.

In the studio, I backed my choices. When you're making music, you're creating something out of nothing. There are a million different ways you could go and choices you could make. That can be overwhelming – especially if you're not allowed to choose what you like, as I had experienced. Instead of getting caught up in never-ending possibilities, I started to make decisions based purely on what I liked. I liked having jazzier, more complex chords because they were interesting to me and felt more emotional. Pop music could feel quite restrained because it was all about being cool. I wasn't concerned with being cool, I was concerned with connecting with people and communicating to them. With my lyrics, I knew I wanted them to be written in a certain, quite specific way. I didn't want them to be super poetic, I wanted to express things the way they are.

After *I Hear a Song*, I had one album left on my contract with Sony. Before we entered negotiations about the album, I made a single with Michael Tan and Andy Mak, who is a very good producer and who had worked with Vera Blue on her incredible debut album, *Perennial*. Together, we wrote a track called 'Crying Underwater', which is a special song for me for a number of different reasons. For one: I didn't have a breakdown in the writing session and end up crying in the bathroom. It had been a long road for me coming back to writing about the things I wanted to write about again, and when we wrote 'Crying Underwater', I felt like I'd reached my destination. I'd worked with Michael on the Carpenters project and had toured with him in the past as well, so even though we'd never written together before, we had a close relationship.

Before we went into the studio for our session, we spoke about a friend and fellow musician who had recently died by suicide. We were both in shock and couldn't believe it. Our friend had seemed really happy, but he must have been struggling underneath. In my conversation with Michael, we spoke about how hard it is for men to talk about their emotions and their challenges. And that's how 'Crying Underwater' came to life. In the studio, I sang and played the piano and Andy made suggestions to tweak certain parts to make it sound incredible. It's a power anthem of a song, and there's something unique about the sound. The opening verse cuts deep ...

I'm surrounded by people
Why do I feel so alone? (Why do I feel so alone?)
Wondering how do I disappear
I just laugh and play along (play along)
I wanna be free but I'm a slave to the voices, the
*   echo in my head*
They make it look so easy
But my body's a graveyard that buries all of my
*   emotions*

The song might have been about my lost friend, but it could well have been about me on a number of occasions.

When we wrote 'Crying Underwater', I really needed to make something I was happy with – and that's exactly what we did. It was a reminder of how satisfying the creative process could – and should – be. The tortured artist trope never applied to me. I think it's a really romantic notion but it's a myth. I can't write when I'm in pain and I don't think you need to be miserable to be a good artist. I think hardships and pain are very much a part of life and it helps if the artist has experienced them to be able to create something that is relatable and deeply meaningful, but for me, if I'm in the middle of going through something horrible, I can't sit and write. If I did, I would sink into a dark hole and have to fight to see the light on the other side. When I'm in the trenches, I can't turn my challenges into something creative. It's only when I'm out of that space and have had time to process that I can look back and reflect on what I've been through.

As I was dealing with the loss of my friend and working on 'Crying Underwater', Ken was in talks with Sony. He pleaded my case for an originals album: I'd done a covers album with *I Hear a Song*, and now I wanted to do something new. Fair's fair.

'Oh, no way, she's definitely going to do another covers record,' was the reply from Sony. Ken kept fighting, but it was no use. As always, Sony had the final say.

'She's either doing a covers record, or she's off the label,' they said.

It was the sentence I'd been waiting for. Ken booked in a meeting. They wanted to see me, and I wanted to talk to them. I entered the boardroom at Sony to find them flanked by lawyers and men in suits. I had Ken beside me, but we were outnumbered. As soon as we sat down at the boardroom table, they talked for twenty minutes non-stop. They insisted that they had my best interests at heart, they told me they wanted to look after me and they pointed out how much they had done for me. They didn't ask me what I wanted. When it was finally my turn to speak, I was very polite.

'Thank you for all that you have done for my career. It's been amazing and I really appreciate it,' I said, calmly. 'But I've heard from your people that if I don't do a covers record, I'm off the label. I feel like I cannot do another covers record for my career. It's just not going to work. I need to explore my original music and my songwriting, so I guess this is it. Thank you.'

I watched their faces drop. They weren't expecting me to call their bluff. They were expecting me to roll over in front of them and their men in suits and do as I was told. This meeting wasn't about covers versus originals – it was about power.

There was some scrambling from their side of the table. They kept assuring me that they knew what was best for me, and when I refused to give up on doing something original, they told me they'd find me a hit song. 'We know a hit song when we hear one, we'll find you an original that will chart,' they said.

I knew exactly what that meant. When Sony said they were going to find me a hit original single, what they actually meant was that they were going to pretend to work on finding me a song, while saying no to every idea I came up with and stalling my career in a never-ending holding pattern.

The waiting game began, and I could see my future at Sony dragging on and on. While I went to writing sessions, Ken kept on talking to the company. He told them that I was happy to be off the label because I didn't feel like the company believed in me or my music. He also hinted that if Sony forced me to put out a covers album to fulfil the last record on my contract, that things could turn nasty. He mentioned the possibility of speaking to the media. That got their attention. The company cared about their reputation.

After all the talking in all the meetings, a deal was struck. Sony wouldn't pick up the option for my last record, but I would stay with their distribution company. I would remain independent for a year and release my music using my own money and their distribution branch without any input, interference, or help from them. The idea was to save them face by preventing me from signing with another label straightaway and becoming successful.

There was a date in the diary. Even after the plan was put forward, Sony could have still backflipped on it. They had up until May 2019 to make their decision. If they wanted to, they could have chosen to pick up the option of my last album and shelve it, letting my career collect dust in the corner. We waited with bated breath until the date passed and they could no longer pick up the option.

On 13 September 2019, I released 'Crying Underwater' as an independent artist. The response was electric. A YouTube user with the account name 'Dami Army Official' posted a beautiful comment on my music video for the song. 'The Queen returns! After so many years since *X Factor* you are now the musician you wanted to be rather than making a song for the sake of being played on the radio. You write songs with depth and heart, and we need more of this today – both in the music industry and the world: songs with meaningful lyrics and singers who feel their words,' they wrote.

'Crying Underwater' was just the start. I followed it up with two more independent singles: 'Marching On' and 'Kiss You Anyway'. The process of writing those songs was entirely different from the way I had been working. At Sony, they would fly me from Brisbane, where I lived, to their Sydney studio to work with writers and producers of their choosing, using their equipment, and taking their lead. When I started doing things on my own, I wrote from home and with different people. I was so used to co-writing with people who I didn't connect with, I almost couldn't remember how to do it. Being able to write with people I felt comfortable with and in safer surroundings helped me to find my creativity again.

As I was stepping out on my own, Ken was stepping out alongside me. After more than a decade at Sony, Ken left the label to run his own management agency, Maven Artist Agency. Of course, I kept Ken on as my manager. We were a team and I trusted him completely.

While I was working on new music and running out the year Sony had forced me to be without a label, Ken was setting up meetings for when the time came that I could sign with someone else. It was Ken who first floated the idea of ABC Music. He'd had other artists on their books and knew that they operated quite differently from Sony. For example, when we were working on a video treatment for a music clip at Sony, the head of the label would have final say and full approval. At ABC, they would defer to the artist, more along the lines of: 'If you're happy, we're happy. Go for it.'

Meeting Natalie Waller, the Head of ABC Music and Events, was another different experience. For one, she was much younger than any other executives I'd worked with (who had all been of a certain generation and male). She was also really respectful, which I liked. I had a good feeling about ABC.

Of course, there are pros and cons to working with small labels and big ones. When I was with Sony, I had the power of a big engine behind me, but I wasn't allowed to drive it. What's the point of a big engine if it doesn't work? Meanwhile, at the ABC, there was a smaller engine, but I would be in control of steering it – and I didn't need to go against what I actually wanted to do, to get the keys.

With more power comes more responsibility. When we started working with ABC in 2020, Ken and I had to do so many things ourselves that we hadn't done before. We got the artwork ready for social media posts, registered songs and found people to help us with radio station promotions. I learned a lot during that process. I'd only ever known one way of doing things – the Sony way – which seemed a mystery to me most of the time, so it was refreshing to see and understand how things actually worked.

I certainly felt like I was at the right point in my life, where I felt strong enough and independent enough to create a career that I would actually enjoy and love in the way that I wanted. There was a sense of 'everything happens for a reason', and that this was the right time and right place for me. But at the same time, there was also some resentment. It was a shame that I had to go through all the mess, all the years of wasted opportunities and all the frustrations I'd been through. I had felt so stuck for so long. I remember having conversations with Noah wishing I could go back to my old life, singing at my church, rather than having the kind of career that I was, which felt like it was all pressure, frustration and powerlessness. I could feel it killing my spirit. It had made me not want to sing, and I loved to sing more than anything else. I know some artists might be okay with having their career led by others and their music chosen for them, but I needed my autonomy.

It wasn't just having to sing what I was told to sing. Even if it's a great song, if it isn't your choice, it's hard to enjoy something you're forced to do. And it's even harder to then have to try to sell that to the public. Having to tell people why a song meant so much to me and how much I loved it – when I had no choice in singing it – was the worst. I was in a difficult position where I was the one who had to sell music which I didn't have a say in. When I did back-to-back promo interviews, I tried to find some kernel of truth so I could sell that as my vision. But when I was inevitably criticised for doing *another* covers album, I couldn't say anything. It made me so angry.

I know those experiences made me grow as a person and an artist though, so I tried to focus on that growth instead of the resentment. I might have been able to get to this place earlier, but I couldn't change the past to speed things up. To go from a place of helplessness to one of excitement was a huge shift. I was grateful to get to that place. The day I could finally sign on as an artist at ABC Music was a good day.

More than anything, I felt lucky to still have a career and to have the opportunity to make exciting music. I was surrounded by amazing people – including Ken, my team at the ABC, the co-writers and producers I worked with, and my friends and family – who were helping me to bring my vision to life. I was very aware that my career could have just fizzled out. I could have given up all together; that's not uncommon.

At ABC Music, I felt empowered. Even so, going into a co-writing session was stressful for me in the early days. There's no set way of approaching a writing session – it's not as though we put aside ten minutes to chat, I write the melody, the co-writer does the lyrics and we come together at the end in a scheduled routine – so every time I'd have to prepare mentally for what might happen. I did – and still do – find it daunting. The more I've co-written and the more I've become used to being in control of choosing the co-writer, the more comfortable I've become. I'm the type of person who likes to have as much information about a situation as possible. Spontaneity freaks me out. I think that's partly why Sony's speed-dating version of session writing didn't work for me. Being thrown in the deep end of songwriting left me floundering, I didn't swim gracefully to the side of the pool; I could barely float.

Because I didn't have any serious music industry experience before *The X Factor* and because I was so sheltered at Sony, I hadn't really had the opportunity to talk to other artists about their writing process. It was only recently that I spoke to another Brisbane-based band who shared their own horror story about a co-writing session in Los Angeles that was a total bust. The band had gone into the session with a famous producer to find the studio packed with nine people and an already completed song. When the producer played the song for them, they didn't get it – and they didn't like it. They tried to put it gently and tell the producer that they were hoping to do something from scratch – explaining that they were a band who created their own music –

but the producer left, upset. Only a couple of the nine people in the studio stayed behind to do the co-writing session, and in the end the band didn't use the song they worked on that day on their album. The entire session was a waste of time. It was a relief for me to hear that I wasn't the only one who struggled in some co-writing situations and that I wasn't alone or absurd for wanting to play a role in the creative process.

* * *

I thought the day might never come but it did – and sooner than I would have thought. In 2021, multiple stories from artists to former employees came out, of the mistreatment and the toxic culture within Sony that had been going on for decades. *Four Corners*, a television program on the ABC, followed and revealed some of these stories of unfair treatment. People like me who knew about Sony felt the program touched lightly on some of the milder mistreatment that went on, but it was still a cathartic moment regardless. I did fantasise about a day where I could speak about those painful and frustrating years, but I never thought I would live to see it. The stories becoming public knowledge and Denis stepping down from his position meant that when I shared my experience I would be believed. Other artists who may want to share their experience also don't have to fear being undermined and silenced.

For so many years, men with grey hair and corporate credit cards were the gatekeepers and tastemakers in Australian music. They dictated what new acts could come through, which established musicians were past their heyday and who couldn't sit at their table.

It was interesting – and a tad ironic – that Natalie Waller at ABC Music took over from Denis Handlin as the chair of the Australian Recording Industry Association (ARIA) board in 2021, a year after I left Sony to sign with her. Natalie was the first female chair of the body. Up until 2019, the board had been entirely made up of men. Denis had been on the ARIA board since 1984 – that's four years before I was even born. Denis had been forced to give up his seat in June 2021 after he had stepped down as the CEO of Sony following allegations of discrimination, bullying and harassment in the Australian office.

I wasn't shocked when I heard about the allegations at Sony, but I was surprised that Denis stepped down from his position.

CHAPTER FOURTEEN

Grand Plans

*T*he year 2019 was going to be my year. I had taken back control of my career and with a new team by my side, we had world domination in our sights. That's a joke! But we were trying to make inroads into other territories outside of Australia. I'd started the year with a holiday to Bali, then I came back to Australia to shoot a campaign for L'Oréal, who I was an ambassador for. I played at Carla Zampatti's Grand Showcase runway closing the Melbourne Fashion Festival, before heading over to Papua New Guinea to perform a show for their prime minister in Port Moresby and then returning to do a very wet performance at the football stadium in Townsville for the North Queensland Cowboys NRL season opener.

In April 2019, I travelled to Manila in the Philippines to do a showcase there. I made appearances on all the breakfast television shows and posed in front of the CNN Philippines studio sign with Ken. On the television shows and at the showcase, I got to introduce 'Dreamer' to an entirely new audience. And they loved it. 'There's no better feeling in the world than knowing I have people that really love my music across the ocean,' I wrote at the time.

While I was in the Philippines, I did another ambassador visit with Compassion. I visited Rodney, the little boy Noah and I had been sponsoring in Cabitan. We played with toy trucks, blew bubbles together and posed for cheeky selfies together with his friends. It was incredible to see the difference in Rodney's health, happiness and confidence since we'd started sponsoring him. Once again, my work with Compassion brought it all home and made everything seem worthwhile.

When I returned home to Australia, I joined Human Nature on their national tour, performed 'My Life in Songs' at the Adelaide Cabaret Festival, froze at the Festival of Voices in Hobart, started my 'Dreamer' tour, released 'Crying Underwater', and prepared to head to Korea for the Asia Song Festival. If it sounds like a whirlwind, that's because it was.

In Korea, I got to see all of these hugely popular K-pop artists on stage. Even though I'm not a K-pop artist, somehow I was one of them. I performed 'Crying

Underwater', 'Super Love', and a bunch of my other favourites at the festival and on a number of Korean television shows and radio programs. Being on shows I watched when I was young was so much fun. It's always really exciting for me when I get to do stuff back in Korea. It feels like a big deal, especially knowing my relatives are watching and are excited about seeing me there.

The K-pop scene is very popularised, and it was interesting to see how the acts were treated over there. There's a lot of secrecy and the management teams kind of hide their artists away. Even though I was really excited to be backstage with bands like Stray Kids, Sunmi and other famous names, they were so heavily controlled by their management teams that I couldn't even ask for a photo with them.

As I've mentioned earlier, as a teenager I was a huge fan of Korean pop music before it became a global phenomenon. So when I see how the rest of the world has become obsessed with K-pop I feel proud. I do feel that there is a lot of work to be done in the industry though in terms of creating a healthier culture for the artists and the fans. There's just so much pressure on these young talents and endless competition to survive and look good.

The festival was in the city of Ulsan, which is a few hours' drive south of Seoul. I got there a few days before my performance to rehearse and get settled. I was with Ken and two of my musos. The show was being filmed for TV, so I wanted to have enough time on the ground to feel really ready. When we arrived at the festival location, we were basically the only ones there. The K-pop acts arrived on the morning of the festival by bus. They came wearing full hair and make-up, so they would've woken up at 3 am to get that done, then left Seoul before dawn to arrive at rehearsals in Ulsan at 7 am. In one way it was shocking to see how hard they were being worked – and how early they had to get up. But in another way, it was just exciting to be there among it all.

I have fans in Korea who have followed me since my *X Factor* days through to Eurovision and beyond, but I've never really been able to perform much over there apart from my show at the embassy and TV and radio performances here and there. The Asia Song Festival was the first time that I got to perform in front of a live audience. It went so well, the organisers said they wanted me to come back the following year for this festival and some other festivals they were working on as well.

While I was in Korea, I found a new agent on the ground there and booked in to do a series of shows in 2020. We had an ambitious and exciting plan for the year ahead of us. Those grand plans were dashed. Almost overnight, the near future became unknown. In the same way my plans were cut short by 2020, this chapter was too.

I know we can't predict the future, but it seems that no-one saw 2020 coming.

CHAPTER FIFTEEN

Dancing Shoes

*I*t was like a scene out of a movie. The cameras were rolling, the stage was set, the lights were bright. Celia Pacquola was about to walk out onto the *Dancing with the Stars* floor when production was halted mid-show. The crew had paused filming to listen to an address from the Australian prime minister. We gathered around a screen – celebrities, dancers and crew, sitting, standing and crouching down. Someone turned the audio up loud so we could all hear Scott Morrison's statement on the Covid-19 crisis. 'It's important that we all try to do the right thing to get through this crisis together,' he said.

It was March 2020, and we might have been in a crisis – a global pandemic – but the show had to go on. When the prime minister's address was over, Celia went out and did the cha-cha. It was an intense moment.

None of us knew what was going to happen, so all we could do was carry on.

My training for *Dancing with the Stars* had started six weeks earlier, after I'd been approached to be a contestant on the popular show. I'd been partnered with the professional dancer Shae Mountain, and he moved to Brisbane for that time so we could go to the dance studio and practise every day. The dance studio was a whole new world for me. Let me be honest with you, I'm not much of a dancer. When I was in high school, I desperately wanted to be able to dance and I went along to an audition for my school dance company with a friend, thinking that we'd be taught a routine and get to learn some moves. On the day, I walked into the room and the teachers asked me to show them my routine. I didn't have a routine. And there was no way I could have come up with something on the spot; I didn't have the confidence or the coordination.

The fact is, I'm totally uncoordinated. Growing up, I used to be made fun of for the way I walked! As a performer I move on stage the way I feel it in the moment, but it's far from being able to dance in an elegant way. I didn't even dance at my wedding.

So, when the producers of *Dancing with the Stars* approached me to be on the show, I told them that all I could do was try. I had always wanted to be able to move better – and to work through the embarrassment of my high school dance company 'audition' – so I thought it would be a good opportunity for me to do exactly that. I figured I'd give it a crack and get better along the way.

Suffice to say, my dance training was a steep learning curve. I was a complete novice, so I had a crash course in the basics. Emphasis on 'crash'! Then I was expected to learn and memorise the perfect waltz, cha-cha and rumba. It was very hard and wasn't made easier by the fact that my partner, Shae, was a little bit shorter than me, which meant some moves were kind of awkward and ruled out any lifts. We weren't just training to do a little dance in front of a few people, we were training to compete on a national television show. Physically, it was debilitating. My body ached all over.

When the series actually started, it took more of a mental toll. I would fly down to Melbourne from Brisbane each week to perform my dance and do interviews. We'd fly back the next day and spend the rest of the week training in Brisbane and learning one – or two – new dances. The schedule was gruelling, but it was the feeling of being out of my depth that stung the most. When you're doing something you're talented at, you can be motivated to practise because you know it'll pay off in the end and you'll be praised for it. I'm such a people pleaser and I always want to impress people, but with dancing, I just couldn't. On the dance floor, I always felt like I was below average – no matter how hard I practised. Then I would be judged by a panel of professionals and the criticism would be aired on television for all to see. Every week, the judges would tell me I didn't do a great job, but every week I kept getting through to the next round. I had the support of my fans and the Dami Army, who were voting to keep me in the competition.

It might sound dramatic because I'm talking about a dancing show, but the training actually triggered some childhood insecurities in me. Shae was a lovely guy, but I could tell when he was frustrated that I couldn't do a certain move or when he thought I wasn't trying hard enough. I was trying as hard as I could, but some things were physically impossible for me to do. Like all the professional dancers, Shae wanted to win, but I wasn't winning material, and I felt bad about that.

In those moments, I felt like I was a child again, being told off by my dad, who had a short fuse when I was growing up. One day I reached my limit and didn't think I could go on. It got so bad I actually wished to get properly injured so I didn't have to train or perform again. How awful is that!? Looking back, I feel silly for taking it so seriously, but at the time it forced me to do some deep soul searching.

The thing that really helped me was talking to the other contestants. It was a similar story with everyone. We were all trying our very best, but even so, none of us were professional dancers. There were lots of tears backstage. People who you wouldn't expect to burst out crying had emotional breakdowns. I think it was quite dramatic for everyone, which is funny because all we were doing was dancing! But it was a vulnerable space to be in, under a lot of pressure, completely exhausted, in the eye of the public, doing something completely foreign. Knowing I wasn't the only one struggling made me feel better, so too did the support of the audience.

In the first weeks of the show (before the pandemic changed everything), we were performing to a live audience in the studio, which was a really good thing for me. Their support helped me do better. I tried not to think about all the people down the camera lens watching me on the television at home and focused on the energy of the live audience instead. When Covid-19 restrictions came in and we stopped having a live audience, it was a totally different vibe. I was performing to a camera instead of a crowd and I knew I was being analysed for every technical move, rather than the show I was putting on.

It was early days of the pandemic and as such, quite a dramatic and confusing time where none of us knew what would happen the next moment. If somebody from the crew or the cast caught the virus, we might all become close contacts and the show might be called off. At one point we had one of the celebrity contestants, Christian Wilkins, become a close contact of someone who had contracted Covid and he and his professional dance partner, Lily, had to isolate and train inside their tiny hotel room for the whole week. For their live performance, they had to dance on the rooftop of their hotel with the cameras operating remotely and the music blasting from outside speakers. There were other people from surrounding buildings watching the two dance from their balconies. The rest of us watched their live performance from inside the studio and cheered for them, recognising what a bizarre situation we were all in.

After six weeks – including a Viennese waltz, a cha-cha, a contemporary number, two sambas, another waltz, a disco marathon, a tango, a foxtrot and a paso doble – I was eliminated in the semi-finals of the competition. Honestly, it was a relief. I was well and truly ready to go home and have a break. The show had been a crazy-busy hurricane, and I really needed a rest.

Little did I know, I was about to have a much longer rest than I ever intended ...

* * *

My first gig to get cancelled was the 2020 Blues Festival at Byron Bay. It was just the start of the cancellations. When borders started to close around the country, I drove from Brisbane down to New South Wales and stayed in a hotel in case I couldn't get into the state. I was at the hotel for three nights before I realised the show was going to get cancelled. Then I drove all the way home.

Being based in Queensland was a blessing and a curse when the border shut down. It meant I couldn't travel interstate for work, but it also meant I could still do shows around the state because we didn't have the same restrictions as New South Wales and Victoria, which had much higher Covid-19 case numbers than we did. I was grateful to still be able to work. So many people in the music industry – including managers, roadies, musicians and technicians – had to quit their jobs and find work in different industries. I was one of the lucky ones. When things got hard – with cancelled shows, closed borders, slow ticket sales and venue restrictions – I reminded myself that every other artist in the world was going through the same thing. Everyone was struggling.

It was extraordinary to see the industry come together, like it had done so many times before. I did my first ever live-streamed concert – a Eurovision Iso Party – in May, joined live-streamed shows with other artists like the band Sheppard, Kate Ceberano and Dannii Minogue, and hosted a Christmas party for the Dami Army with a festive live-streamed show in December. When times are tough, musicians rally. And that's exactly what we did in 2020. The industry changed overnight, and we changed with it. But underneath the unity and solidarity, there was still fear.

I questioned whether I'd be able to come back from the industry-wide shut-down. I'd spent all of 2019 performing around the world, and I didn't know if I would be able to do that again in the future. 'Am I still going to have a career after all this is over?' I asked myself. Music isn't just my job, it's such a big part of my identity. It's what I've always done and all that I know. There is no alternative for me. The thought of losing that was painful.

It was disappointing and disheartening to have so many gigs cancelled, to see so many venues go bust and to have no certainty about anything, but all we could do was wait it out. Sometimes it feels like I'm still waiting ...

Still, in 2020, I managed to play solo shows in Brisbane, Ipswich, Cairns and on the Gold and Sunshine coasts. I also did my first solo shows in the regional towns of Rockhampton and Bundaberg, and it was awesome being able to perform to new crowds and to see new parts of my state. The solo shows meant I could really engage with the audience. It was just me, my piano and the microphone. I told stories and cracked jokes in between songs, and people really responded to everything I said and did. It was so nice. I was used to having a band and a big sound system behind me, but I'd always wanted to do a smaller, more relaxed, show. The pandemic opened that door for me and pushed me through it. My voice took centre stage with just my keys accompanying me.

As much as I enjoyed it, I knew I couldn't keep solely performing in Queensland, so I announced a small solo tour called 'Piano, Songs and Stories' that was set to kick off in early 2021 when things started to ease up a little. I was just desperate to get out there and play my music. It ended up being a scattered tour, with border restrictions, cancelled shows, postponements and some fortunately timed dates that went ahead. When we planned the tour, we organised a show at the Sydney Opera House, which was going to be the highlight of the whole thing. The tickets sold out in a heartbeat. A night to remember! A moment in time! A career milestone! I was so excited.

Yeah, it didn't happen. My New South Wales dates on the 'Piano, Songs and Stories' tour were cancelled when the state went into another lockdown and restrictions were put in place. Of course it was disappointing, but I tried to count my blessings. I'd been able to perform more than most artists had in the throes of the pandemic; I'd also been able to spend a lot of time working on new music, and I even scored another reality television spot.

In October 2021, I joined the cast of *Celebrity MasterChef*. I love eating food – and sharing Korean food with people – so I thought it would be a good chance to do both. I also think my manager, Ken, had told the producers that I was a really good cook, which might have been a slight exaggeration! Just like the *Dancing with the Stars* stage, the *MasterChef* kitchen was an entirely new experience for me. With *MasterChef*, though, I only had a week and a half to prepare and practise. I was in Sydney at the time and working on new music, so I only ended up having five days to sharpen my cooking skills and perfect my signature dish. I had a handful of dishes up my sleeve ready to pull out for the challenges.

It was interesting to cook next to other celebrity contestants. I tasted Olympic swimmer Ian Thorpe's mac and cheese dish, actress Rebecca Gibney's Thai fried rice and comedian Dilruk Jayasinha's beef rendang. Some were surprisingly very good at cooking, like the famous football player Nick Riewoldt, who was cooking up impressive dishes and who ended up taking out the competition, and others ... not so much. But more than anything it was fun spending time with these interesting people who I wouldn't have had a chance to meet otherwise. I remember going out for dinner with them one weekend, and watching Tilly Ramsay FaceTiming her dad, Gordon Ramsay. It was right then that I knew I was in trouble. Everyone started to share who they were friends with and getting advice from – they happened to be names of famous chefs you would know if I named them here.

I was getting advice from my people too but they happened to be my mum and Ken. Mum's always been a great cook at home, always overfeeding the whole family, but her specialty is Korean food, which is very different from the challenges we were set. Ken doesn't even know how to fry an egg so he was useless for cooking tips. I would ask for advice like, 'What should I cook this week?' And they would say, 'I don't know.' I made Korean dishes like Dolsot bibimbap and Doenjang soup and even impressed myself with how well they turned out. I liked being able to share my culture through food, but also I thought if I make Korean dishes that no-one knows about they won't be able to criticise me. Normally I don't put a lot of effort into the presentation of the things I cook, but I made the dishes look really good. And I swear no-one helped me with them! The dishes I planned – like banquet noodles and a kimchi pancake, a tornado kimchi fried omurice and the Dolsot bibimbap – didn't last very long. When I ran out of go-to recipes, I tried to do a cheesecake. Big mistake. I'm not a dessert maker, and not surprisingly, I stuffed it up. I was eliminated in the second week of the competition. An undercooked sweet potato Basque cheesecake was my undoing. Unlike *Dancing with the Stars*, where I was relieved to be finally eliminated and freed from my misery, I was quite disappointed to be going home as I would have loved to have spent more time on this show playing with food and being with the amazing people, and even trying to win.

I flew home to Brisbane promising everyone that I would be back for the finale to celebrate and to say goodbye to everyone. Unfortunately, though, Covid lockdowns hit again and I wasn't able to fly to Melbourne and join everybody else.

When I got home I was back in the new uncertain world of Covid, not knowing for how long the ever-changing restrictions would continue and if we were going to face more disappointments, but I was filled with a new passion to cook and try making different dishes. And I realised with the lockdowns I might even have time to master a perfect Basque cheesecake or try that delicious carbonara recipe.

CHAPTER SIXTEEN

A New Reality

*T*here's a saying: sometimes in a room full of people, you can feel the most alone. That's the kind of feeling I was trying to capture when I sat down with the songwriter Garrett Kato at his home studio in Byron Bay. Garrett is an artist in his own right and is well respected in the folk-pop scene. As soon as we met, we clicked. He was really nice and easy to talk to – and he understood the highs and lows of being in the music business. We chatted about how the longer you're in this industry, the more you tour and the more famous you get, the lonelier you feel. That feeling was something we both related to, and it was nice to have that connection with someone.

After *The X Factor* and then Eurovision, so many things in my life got bigger, including the pressures put on my shoulders, but also the size of the platform I could use to help others and the opportunities I was exposed to. Other things got smaller, namely my circle of community. I became closer with my close friends and drifted away from friends who were more like acquaintances. A lot of people didn't understand what I was going through. It was hard for me to attend things in big group settings, because I didn't want to be recognised, or treated differently, or be the centre of attention. I certainly didn't want to be given any celebrity treatment.

It was in Garrett's studio surrounded by trees and the lushness of the Byron hinterland that these feelings spilled out onto the page and across the keys of the piano. The result was 'Alone'. When we wrote this song in 2020, we didn't know exactly how alone we'd all be in the thick of the Covid-19 pandemic.

Almost overnight, Zoom replaced face-to-face meetings for me – and everyone else – and my co-writing sessions went online. After years of dreading my writing sessions, doing them over Zoom eased me back into the practice. Being in the safety of my own home and having the ability to get up and make a cup of coffee for myself as I was writing made me feel comfortable. I felt less threatened working with somebody on a screen than I did when I had a stranger sitting next to me in a studio. So while a lot of people were complaining about having to use Zoom, I was enjoying it.

I reached out to a producer named Andrew Burford (who's also known as One Above), who had worked extensively with hip-hop legends Hilltop Hoods. His sound is really interesting and has a mix of hip-hop and R&B influences which I've always favoured and I loved the idea of having his input in my music. So in my very first Zoom co-writing session, I logged on with Andrew and Bri Clark, who is a Perth-based singer-songwriter. From the comfort of my home studio, I told them I wanted to write a song about a cactus. Not just any cactus, a lonely cactus. I had come up with a chorus idea, a simple melody and words 'I'm a lonely cactus' with some chords underneath. As many of my songs do, this one also started at the keyboard, more as a slower, sad feel. I sent it across to Andrew and he came back with a number of different directions we could take it in. He suggested various beats and guitar riffs to go with it. I loved it so much. It was such an exciting process. We went back and forth with all of our ideas for the rest of the lyrics and melodies, and made the entire song remotely from three different states and time zones. I recorded all the vocal tracks at home and sent them to Andrew in Sydney, where he compiled everything and sent the song back with his notes. Then I'd send him back new takes and notes from my end – 'let's try this', 'and change that', 'and amp it up here' –

and even though we were hundreds of kilometres apart, it all just came together exactly how it was meant to. It was such an interesting way to work, and for me it felt a lot more natural being able to do my own thing in my own space.

I'd had a studio set up in my home for years – and had invested in quality equipment and soundproofing – but never thought it was good enough to be used on a record. When Covid hit, I didn't have a choice. We soon realised that the vocal quality was actually fine – and it also made the process so much easier. At home, I could do as many or as few takes as I liked, without having to worry about the sound engineer knocking off at 5 pm or forcing myself to push through if I was having a bad day. Of course, the downside to that freedom is that I could do a million takes and still not be happy with any of them. But it's nice to have the option. After the songs are mixed and produced, no-one can tell that the vocals were recorded at home instead of in a professional studio.

When the border between Queensland and New South Wales briefly opened up, I went down to work on another song with Andrew in person in his studio in Sydney. It was a little weird, because we'd already made a song together – 'Lonely Cactus' – but it was the first time we were actually meeting in real life. As strange as it was, we worked together really well (again) and the result was 'Scared to Talk to You', a song about drifting away and growing apart from a close friend. It's a journey of a song, tracking the highs and lows of a friendship.

In a similar way, my songwriting path has definitely been a journey, with accompanying highs and lows. I feel like I'm in a better place now where I can be myself again. I love writing and I love getting to say things through my songs. It's the way it should have been all along.

Now, when I sit down in a co-writing session, I go into it with a sense of security and structure. I'm looking after myself more, and I'm in a much better place with my confidence. I know I work better when I take something with me as a starting point. I've learned that it's less intimidating for me to work with a group of contributors if we start with something that came from me. Then when the co-writers bring in an idea or things that I haven't thought of, it feels exciting. I enjoy hearing other people's suggestions, and having a co-writer makes things move a lot quicker. I no longer spend the whole day agonising over one little section and not knowing which way to take it. Working with others used to strike fear and panic in me, now it inspires me.

* * *

In 2020, I announced I was going to try out for Eurovision again the following year. Since I competed in 2016, SBS had created a show where artists would compete to win the public's vote to represent the country in Europe. I wrote a song called 'Paper Dragon' with Eleanor Witt, who goes by the moniker ELKI, and I thought it could be my Eurovision song for 2021. After my experience in 2016 performing someone else's song, I thought it would be amazing to perform one of my own. Eurovision is interesting because a lot of songwriters compete in the contest, but they often pick a song that they didn't write. That's what I did the first time around. So, when I was laying down the groundwork for my second shot, I knew I wanted to be involved as a writer as well as the performer.

In the Chinese Zodiac, I was born in the Year of the Dragon – and there was something about the song 'Paper Dragon' that felt meant to be. Eleanor had come up with a quirky melody and lyric idea that really stood out as a song, and we wanted to turn it into something epic and powerful. In my mind, the song was all colour and fun and magic.

When it came to making the video clip for the song, that's exactly what I wanted to bring to life. I ended up working with an Italian artist named Stefano Bertelli, but the collaboration almost never happened. Stefano had sent an email to Ken with a link to his paper-made stop-motion animation work, but it ended up in Ken's spam folder. Somehow Ken stumbled across it among his 'junk' emails and forwarded it to me. My reaction to his work was: 'This is really interesting and different.' We got in touch with Stefano, and I explained my vision for the song 'Paper Dragon', and together we came up with a brief. Stefano made the whole video using paper cut-outs, including a world with a giant dragon – he literally sat down for hours cutting and folding them together – and then he filmed them and used animation to bring them to life. It was extraordinary, and he did it all from Italy, on the other side of the world from me.

As I said, I had been hoping to take the song 'Paper Dragon' to Europe for Eurovision in 2021, but because the song contest was cancelled in 2020 for the first time in its over sixty-year history, Montaigne ended up being our representative the following year. Montaigne had won *Eurovision: Australia Decides* in 2020 with her song 'Don't Break Me', but she never got to perform it on the world stage because the competition was cancelled. It was only fair she should get the opportunity to live her Eurovision dream. In the end she wasn't able to attend in person in 2021 due to the continuing restrictions, but sent in her performance remotely.

With Eurovision off the cards, I decided to go ahead and release 'Paper Dragon' as a single because it was something different and exciting – and the world desperately needed something fun. Along with 'Alone', 'Lonely Cactus' and 'Scared to Talk to You', 'Paper Dragon' formed the base of my fifth studio album – and my very first album with ABC Music. I decided to call the album *MY REALITY*. In the time since I'd left Sony, my reality had changed so much, I wanted to acknowledge and mark that.

Then Ken sent me a message he'd received: 'Hey, Audius is keen to work with Dami. He's very picky with who he works with, so it should be great.' In the past, Audius Mtawarira had worked with Jess Mauboy, Delta Goodrem, Flo Rida and Ludacris. Our co-writing session was in person in Sydney. As usual, I had my standard nerves about working with someone new who I'd never met before, but I knew I was capable of dealing with whatever happened on the day. We agreed on a studio and a time, and I walked up into the building. Whenever I walk into a new session, we sit down and start talking about all sorts of topics to try to get to know the other person. Sometimes there is an easy connection where you know that you are both on the same wavelength. Other times, you feel like they're not really getting you. As soon as I met Audius I felt super relaxed and comfortable. He is very softly spoken and humble, the type of person I like to work with. The pandemic was at the front of everyone's minds at the time, and so our conversation got really deep really fast. Everyone was freaked out about the state of the world and no-one knew what was going to happen. It was all incredibly unsettling.

I arrived at the session thinking that I didn't want an inspiration song, I wanted to make something light and upbeat. But as Audius and I started talking, our conversations turned deeper, even spiritual, even though we'd just met.

We agreed that all of us needed a message of hope to hold on to, something inspirational to encourage people to keep going. We were all feeling heavy and out of sorts.

We started with a melody and lyrics for the first verse that painted a chaotic and dark landscape, which is exactly how our world felt.

People rushing by, bright city lights
As I look down from my hotel room
Angry cars and lonely hearts
Guess they're tryna get home soon

Hallelujah, Hallelujah
Can we stop and take a breath?
Maybe we just need to pray
Hallelujah, Hallelujah
When it's more than we can take
It's time for us to pray
Hallelujah

I was playing the piano while we were tossing around ideas for the chorus. There were a few different ideas but none of them really felt right. I said to him, 'I want something simple and explosive. I don't know what it is but it has to be something like "Hallelujah, Hallelujah".' I didn't mean to put those words in there but Audius said, 'That's it.' Those words gave the song the life it needed – almost as if we were taking it to church – and that's how the track 'Pray' came about. I left the studio that day feeling energised and excited about what we had created. Sometimes that feeling lasts until the next morning when you listen back to what you made and realise it was questionable. But after that session, the feeling stuck. I liked the song and when I played it to a few other people, including Ken, they liked it even more than I did, which is always a positive sign. 'Pray' became the first song on the track list of my yet-to-be-released album.

I worked with many different co-writers and producers on the album. They all had very unique sounds and styles – from hip-hop to Triple J folk to party pop anthems – so consistency could have been a concern. It could have been, but it wasn't. The one thing every track had in common? It was my vision. This was going to be the first album where I had control over the whole process so I listened to each track to make sure that the whole album was threaded with my overall plan and my style of storytelling. My voice came through clearly, production was organic and minimalistic, chords and arrangements sounded good, and I wasn't trying to please other people. I had a clear idea of what I wanted the album to be – and what I didn't want it to be – and I had the power to tell the producers and the mixing engineer and even the photographer and designers exactly what needed to happen to get it where I wanted.

I released *MY REALITY* on 29 October 2021. I couldn't wait. I was excited to get the album out and to tour it and then to get straight back into it and write another one. That didn't happen. The album dropped just before the new Omicron variant started to spread in Australia, so while we had intended to do live shows and had dates booked in, they were cancelled. It was sad that we didn't get to take the album on the road and perform it in front of audiences, but looking back, I still would have pushed ahead with releasing *MY REALITY*. I needed it to be out in the world, and I like to think other people might have needed it too.

This was my first record since parting with Sony and it was made up entirely of original songs. I'd poured my heart and soul into every single track, every lyric, and every melody. In its first week, the album reached number two on the Australian Albums chart and topped the Australian Indie album chart. This result meant more to me than anyone could have known.

The response to and success of the album filled my heart with joy and pride and sweet satisfaction. For so many years I had doubted my ability as a songwriter – and had been denied so many opportunities to write my own songs – so having my original work celebrated was a triumph.

There were plenty of times when I felt like giving up, and at the end of the day I would have always written my own songs and performed them even if it was back at where I started, at a church with ten people in the audience. But I made it here, and I still had an army of supporters who waited for me and my music – pun intended for the Dami Army, of course. A whole eight years and four albums later, I'd finally made my dream album, with songs I actually love and want to listen to.

This was truly a milestone and I had many teary moments just thinking about the journey it had taken to get to this point.

What's that saying? The best revenge is success …

CHAPTER SEVENTEEN

It's Only Just Begun

When my plan to try out for the 2021 Eurovision Song Contest was cancelled by the pandemic, I assumed I'd just give it a go the following year. I had already started planning and preparing for my second run at Eurovision for 2022 when I found out that I was pregnant. We weren't actively trying to have a baby but we said that we were ready for it if it were to happen. And we got lucky.

I knew we were fortunate to be in this position, but I went through such complex emotions. They were similar feelings to those I had before my wedding day, aged twenty-four. On one hand I was looking forward to marrying someone I loved and starting a new chapter of my life. On the other hand, I was so afraid of how my life would change, mainly from people who would treat me differently and put me into a box that I didn't fit into. I hated being pushed into the married-woman stereotype and being excluded from my friends. For almost ten years, people were asking me about my 'baby plans' like that's what I was expected to do next. Complete strangers would ask me about my pregnancy instead of my music, as though that was what I was famous for.

But I wasn't the same person I was back then. I was no longer in my early twenties and afraid to speak up when I had to. I've been through a lot more since that time and knew better than to spend too much energy worrying about the way people behaved towards me. I knew it would still annoy the crap out of me when people put me into the stereotype of babies and mums and lullabies when I'm still the same person I was last year. But I also knew not to focus on that but on myself and my values.

When the baby arrived, it was a completely new world that surprised me. When I saw his face for the first time as he was put on my body seconds after birth, I cried as my heart filled with a kind of love that I'd never felt before. Prior to this when parents would gush about falling in love with their child, their babies being perfect etc. I thought it sounded so narcissistic! Like confessing love to the mirror. Of course you love your own child, they look like you!

But when I saw little Harry I felt exactly the same way, and I couldn't help myself. It was a complete clichéd moment but clichés exist for a reason – because they are so universal. Was it the hormones? Was it the mystery of God? I fell in love with this stranger who seemed to have appeared out of nowhere and I felt like I wanted to protect him with everything I had. A little person who is so vulnerable and so perfect at the same time.

When we found out that we were having a boy, I came up with the name Harrison, Harry for short, and the middle name would be after his dad's English name, Noah, which was the name I found for my husband in the first place. We asked Noah's mum in Korea to help come up with a Korean name and she suggested Jiho, meaning a wise tiger, as he was born in the Year of the Tiger. I loved that his name gave him connections to our family here, and family back in Korea as well.

When I shared the news on social media, I got a huge reaction of people congratulating me and Noah. Getting to this new phase in life opened me up to a new world. I gained an insight into families and the love parents feel for their children. I now understood how my parents might have felt for me throughout my life – how worried they would have been seeing me struggle, and how proud they would have felt for every one of my achievements big and small. I started to notice so many people with prams and babies on the streets. The sleepless nights parents went through! The love and the joys they feel. And also the heartbreak, tiredness and the boredom. The roller-coaster of emotions.

At the same time, just as I had suspected, there were people trying to put me into a new box: 'You're a mum now.' People looked at me with suspicion, as though I wasn't the same person I had been before I gave birth. People became wary about whether I would honour my commitments to perform and work, and they were hesitant to book me onto shows. People assumed I would just change. That I would go and take a break or even retire.

I was glad that I waited till I was ready and in my thirties. I was better equipped to process such a big life change, and it definitely has been a life-changing event. I have a better understanding of myself and what is important to me. I can't help but occasionally worry about the opinions of strangers but only for a short while. I know what really matters to me and how to focus on my priorities and the opinions of only those who love and care for me. I know in my soul that I am still myself, even with a new baby in my life whom I love with all my heart.

Eurovision takes place in May, and that was my due date for Harry. The timing meant that I had to postpone plans for Eurovision once again. As in 2020, I had big things lined up for the next couple of years all centred around Eurovision, which had to be readjusted. But I couldn't stand the thought of not having anything planned for the next year.

While I was pregnant, I started to write this book, which has been a project that has given me so much insight and understanding about myself and the road I've been on. It's been cathartic to write down what I've been through from the beginning to this point; processing the pain and the challenges that I have overcome; to relive those moments of triumph; to remember visiting Compassion children in remote villages around the world and how that's always been a dream and a calling of mine. To be reminded of how many shows I've done around Australia and around the world and how meeting my fans, the Dami Army, made me feel. I have managed to fit in so much over the years that I had forgotten some of it. Being reminded of those highs and lows has made me realise the strength that I have in me and how far I have come.

Some asked, 'Aren't you a bit too young to be writing a memoir?' But it's been a good time for me to reflect and breathe and really think about what I want to do with my life and my career. Until now, I was always going from one project to another, and had no time to stop and think about the bigger-picture goals and vision.

Next year will be the tenth year of my official solo career and also marks ten years since meeting the Dami Army. I have so many plans – this book, more music and other projects – that make my heart beat a million miles an hour that I would love to continue with. I will continue to explore and follow my dreams like I have been doing, whatever that may look like.

Acknowledgements

emories of events are subjective and can vary from person to person. This is my version of the stories that I share with others. I thank the people who also share these memories with me, for generously allowing me to tell my story.

To tell my story of finding my voice, I have had to focus on certain parts of my journey and leave out others. That meant I had to withhold important moments and chapters of my life involving friends and family whom I dearly love. I hope you understand.

Thank you to Sophie Hamley and the team at Hachette for believing that my story was worth telling and helping me through my first book. I wouldn't have enjoyed it as much without your kind and effective guidance. Also to Jacquie Brown for helping me shape my words and sentences to convey what's actually in my heart.

Thank you to my manager and Harry's godfather, Ken, for protecting my flame so that I could write with courage and truth.

Thank you to my husband, Noah, who gives me reason and power to pursue my dreams to the fullest. You have an incredible life story of your own (which I know you will get to write and share one day) and my journey is shaped and inspired by yours.

Thank you to my mum and dad for being the village for Harry so that I could keep making music and finish writing this book. I definitely couldn't have done everything without your help.

hachette
AUSTRALIA

If you would like to find out more about
Hachette Australia, our authors, upcoming events
and new releases you can visit our website or our
social media channels:

hachette.com.au
HachetteAustralia
HachetteAus